HUGO L. BLACK

A STUDY IN THE JUDICIAL PROCESS

LONDON: GEOFFREY CUMBERLEGE
OXFORD UNIVERSITY PRESS

HUGO L. BLACK

A STUDY IN THE JUDICIAL PROCESS

By

CHARLOTTE WILLIAMS

BALTIMORE

THE JOHNS HOPKINS PRESS

1950

PRINTED IN THE UNITED STATES OF AMERICA
BY J. H. FURST COMPANY, BALTIMORE, MARYLAND

PREFACE

The year 1937 marked the beginning of a new period in the history of the Supreme Court of the United States. It was in that year that the Court began its retreat from its long-held position of general hostility to the expansion of governmental power and showed signs of falling in step with a newly ascendant school of political thought. It was likewise in that year that President Roosevelt had the opportunity to make his first appointment to the Supreme Court, whereupon, with the selection of Hugo L. Black of Alabama, the "Roosevelt Court" began to take shape. Although Black's appointment did not mark the precise chronological point from which the Court's philosophy began its deviation from its previous path, it was this event which made it plain beyond all doubt that the Court was about to be reconstituted in the image of the New Deal.

There is always danger that the recorder of current annals, lacking advantage of perspective, may assign to recent events an importance quite out of proportion to their true place in history. Yet it seems safe to assert that the thirteen years from Blacks' appointment to the present have been extraordinarily significant ones in the development of constitutional interpretation. Never in so short a period has the Court so frequently and drastically reversed previous positions.

While a study of the work of a single justice, albeit an influential one, can but partially reflect movements in the mainstream of juristic thought, it is nevertheless true that an under-

v

standing of such movements demands a consideration of the opinions and philosophies of the individual members of the Court. As a step toward such an understanding I have herein undertaken an examination of the official career of the first Roosevelt appointee to the Supreme Court. If such a study may serve as a contribution to a general appraisal of the trend and temper of constitutional theory during a stormy decade of the Court's history its purpose will have been accomplished.

To Dr. Carl B. Swisher of The Johns Hopkins University I owe an immeasurable debt of gratitude. It was in his classes that my interest in the Supreme Court and its work was first kindled and throughout the course of the present study he gave generously of his time and counsel. I am also indebted to Dr. V. O. Key who read the entire manuscript and offered a number of helpful criticisms. My father, Albert Williams, and Judge S. L. Felts of the Tennessee Court of Appeals contributed much by their comments upon judicial opinions from the viewpoint of professional lawyers.

CHARLOTTE WILLIAMS

TABLE OF CONTENTS

CHAPTER I

THE APPOINTMENT

Never were auspices less favorable than those under which Hugo LaFayette Black in October 1937 began his career as an Associate Justice of the Supreme Court of the United States. The appointing power had but lately suffered its worst political setback; his selection had been a surprise determined upon with little or no advice from political leaders; and few persons who were regarded as able to measure professional attainment thought him equipped for his task either by training or temperament. Added to this there was unearthed from his past the skeleton of membership in the Ku Klux Klan, whereupon such a storm of protest broke as is seldom seen even in a mercurial democracy.

The issue upon which the administration had been so thoroughly defeated was the so-called, "court packing plan," whereby the President would have been empowered to add to the Supreme Court six new justices whose political predilections were favorable to the principles and policies of the New Deal. It should be noted that this proposal did not generate all the opposition which it occasioned. Like all political leaders who break with the traditions of a long-accepted social order or threaten the privileges of entrenched power, President Roosevelt had alienated the conservatives of the country and stirred hatreds far deeper than those which ordinarily result from partisan politics. When his plan to enlarge the Court was announced it seemed to his enemies that the

1

day of his downfall was foreshadowed and that their opportunity to discredit the New Deal was at hand.

In 1932 the conservative element in the United States had not felt greatly put out by the Democratic victory. Philosophically enough their spokesmen seemed willing to accept the defeat of President Hoover as a rebuke that would teach Republican administrations to be more careful thereafter. The minority party had been employed for such chastening purposes in the past with no permanent ill effects either to the country or to the Republican party, and everyone was accustomed to praise the two-party system under which an organized opposition stands by to threaten those in power with the possibility of overthrow if they too far forget public interest or too clumsily execute the prerogatives of office. Most Republicans took it for granted that no Democratic success since the Civil War had resulted from popular approval of the principles of the Democratic party, but only from dissatisfaction with particular Republican regimes, and they knew no reason why this condition should not continue far into the future. After all, most of the people of the country were Republicans—a comforting thought in the hours of temporary defeat.

The conservatives of both parties believed that the people of the United States were well satisfied with their political and economic systems and did not consider that a change of the party in power was likely to threaten the destruction of either. Populists and Socialists who held views antagonistic to the established order had appeared at times, but generally they were almost as unwelcome among those who dominated the Democratic councils as among the Republicans. Chronic complainers were expected to appear occasionally against whom each party would shut its doors and who were too few to attain much headway under their own power.

Moreover the new President, although a Democrat, was a New Yorker. Better still, he was no parvenu who had clambered up the political ladder from the city slums, but an aristocrat of good Dutch lineage, bred upon the banks of the Hudson and living upon an old fortune still intact. Since his family funds would be quick to suffer from confiscatory taxes or a cycle of low return on invested capital, it was natural to expect that he would understand almost instinctively the arguments against distributism or the lodgment of too much power in the hands of the proletariat. There was nothing in his record to indicate that he was not sound where the protection of property was involved, or even that he was very radical where the issue was the preservation of certain good old-fashioned means of acquiring it.

The President lost little time in disillusioning those who reasoned in this manner. Within three months after taking office he persuaded Congress to devalue the currency, an action that struck 41 cents from every gold dollar in the country and repudiated the government's promise to redeem its currency in a particular medium. On the ground that desperate diseases require desperate remedies and that the economic malady from which the country was suffering could be checked only by strong medicine, the President recommended this act. The Court's action in sustaining it caused Justice James C. McReynolds to say, "The Constitution as many of us have understood it, the instrument that has meant so much to us, is gone." [1]

In quick succession came pronouncements of policy which

3

marked the Roosevelt administration as something new in American history. As the President appealed for statutes to lighten the load or increase the comfort of " the forgotten man," it became apparent that he was a building a following among that portion of the population that had enjoyed little in the past and that he was not averse to capitalizing upon discontent and the prevalence of poverty, not merely by expressions of sympathy, but by recommending to Congress legislation calculated to narrow the spread between the respective living standards of the poor and the well-to-do. Some of his enemies regarded him as an arrant demagogue, some as a socialistic sciolist unimpressed by the importance of the foundations of economic stability. When his plan to alter the political complexion of the Supreme Court was announced the heat already generated broke into crackling blaze.

After his second election many conservatives were convinced that the voters were temporarily deranged and that nothing but the Supreme Court stood between the United States and dangerous radicalism. Even the Court was not a thoroughly reliable bulwark for it was divided rather evenly on many issues and its conservative conclusions were sometimes by narrow margins. Four justices, the conservatives felt, could be counted on to vote on the right side of almost any important question. These were McReynolds, Van Devanter, Butler, and Sutherland. Counted on to vote wrong with considerable regularity upon novel questions of governmental authority were Brandeis, Cardoza, and Stone. In advance of a decision they could never be sure how Roberts should be counted, and even less could they depend upon the vote of Chief Justice Hughes. The former, they thought, showed signs of improving with age, but the latter, whom a couple of Washington newspaper columnists had denominated "The Man on the Flying Trapeze,"[2] had come to cause no surprise by landing on either side of any question involving governmental authority.

Yet for all its uncertainty when confronted with specific issues the Supreme Court was recognized as a thing apart from the New Deal, and conservatives still felt that they could depend upon it should New Deal vagaries too far o'erleap themselves. If the Court had betrayed sound thought and good morals in the gold cases,[3] it had at any rate unanimously declared the National Industrial Recovery Act unconstitutional,[4] disapproved a congressional attempt to pass a compulsory pension act for railroad employees,[5] frowned upon the government's liberality toward debtors in the passage of new bankruptcy legislation,[6] refused to allow federal interference with important problems of relationship between employer and worker,[7] and called a halt upon governmental alleviation of agricultural distress.[8] It might not indeed be the best Court that could be selected, but conservative opinion still thought it was something for which true Americans ought to thank the tutelary Providence that somehow always saves their country in time of peril.

The feeling of the outright New Dealers about the Court was quite as strong in the opposite direction. Ever so often some liberal iconoclast would question the doctrine of judicial review of legislative action and suggest either its re-examination or its restriction. The President himself was no very fervent advocate of this American innovation in government and had let it be known on numerous occasions that he did not hold with those who believed that the Court could do no wrong. In his campaign against Hoover he spoke of the Court as an adjunct of a reactionary administration, and though this remark was said to have been made *ex tempore,* he never apologized for it. The invalidation of the National Industrial Recovery Act had evoked his caustic comment, and each victory for the conservative side of a legal controversy confirmed his opinion that the Supreme Court as constituted was the chief stumbling block in the path of political progress.

When the election of 1936 justified the President's faith that he spoke for the overwhelming majority of the nation's people, he lost little time in undertaking to remove this impediment. By the phenomenal victory in which he won the electoral votes of all the states except Maine and Vermont, he and his fireside advisers were persuaded more than ever before that popular approval would be given almost any project he should sponsor.

It was under these conditions that the President's plan to increase the Court's membership came before the country. It was the method chosen after serious study of other possible means by which the veto power of the Court's conservative members could be ended. Immediately after his second election the President consulted with his Attorney-General, Homer S. Cummings, concerning the most feasible way of dealing with the one department of government which had failed to fall in line with his leadership. Cummings set to work with enthusiasm, digesting the counsel of his trusted subordinates and evaluating the virtues of the various methods that from time to time have been recommended to modify the anomaly that permits a few men holding office for life to say what laws the representatives of the people may enact in a nation which asserts that it is a republic.

The plan least open to criticism was the submission of a constitutional amendment rearranging the machinery of government so that the Supreme Court should not have the final and unchallengeable power to set aside legislative enactments. A provision that Congress might by some particular majority override the judgment of the Court even as it may pass a proposal over the President's veto might have seemed not very unreasonable even to those who opposed it, for it would have been but an extension of the familiar system of checks and balances to reach a situation about which the Constitution was silent. But such a plan was at best a slow one and would have transferred the determination of the issue to forty-eight forums where the influence of national executive power was certain to be less potent than at Washington.

To be sure the Constitution already gave Congress a check upon the Court by permitting it to prescribe the greater part of the Court's jurisdiction, and on one occasion shortly after the Civil War an unpopular decision of the Court had been dealt with by denuding it of jurisdiction in a particular field.[9] This expedient, however, left much to be desired. Instead of making the Court into an ally of the New Deal and a respectable exponent of its principles, such procedure would have left it composed of recalcitrants, powerless perhaps to halt legislation, but able by pious mouthings to render it unpopular and misconstrue its application.

It had also been suggested that Congress was already authorized to say that the Court could act to invalidate legislation only when it did so by unanimous vote or by some named proportion. This dubious authority, however, would have to be tested before the

Court which, without express authority in the Constitution, had claimed the unique right to overthrow legislative enactment, and it might just as plausibly assert a constitutional right to nullify legislation by a bare majority.

The simplest solution as well as the most convenient seemed to be to over-balance the objectionable influence on the Court by increasing its membership. It is human nature to desire to be tried before a friendly judge and it no doubt seemed to the President and his advisers that their worst troubles would be over if men of their own views could be appointed to determine whether they had exceeded their constitutional limitations. So the President and the Attorney-General decided upon what appeared to be the quickest and easiest plan—a bill empowering the President to appoint six new associate justices of the Supreme Court. Besides the Attorney General, few appear to have been taken into the President's confidence until the plan was ready to be made public.

It was easy enough to see the points at which the opposition would direct its attacks. In many quarters the United States Supreme Court has come to be regarded as sacrosanct, a sort of Ark of the Covenant that some extra-constitutional moral authority forbids profane hands to touch. Moreover, for a litigant to demand the right to name his judge is likely to be regarded by the public as something less than sportsmanlike. It was fair to assume that there were some well-informed Americans who were already looking with alarm at the spread of totalitarianism in Europe and who might see in the complete dominance of the executive power an American tendency to follow in that direction.

It is not to be supposed that President Roosevelt and Attorney-

8

General Cummings failed to foresee these difficulties, and there is no reason to suspect that they did not weigh them. Where they erred was in believing that the effect of the several foreseen objections might be minimized by making the prime purpose appear but a part and parcel of a general plan to reorganize the whole federal judicial system along lines of greater efficiency and smoother coordination. As events were later to prove, they were mistaken when they assumed that the Supreme Court issue could be in any measure rendered less arresting to public attention by including it in a bill which effected reasonable and needed reforms in the lower branches of the federal judiciary.

The bill proposed by the President in a message to Congress on February 5, 1937, provided that the executive might appoint an additional judge to serve on any federal court when the occupant of a judicial position had served more than ten years on the bench and had continued to serve more than six months after becoming seventy years of age. It provided that the number of judges on any federal court should be permanently increased by these additions, the inferior courts not to be increased in membership by more than two, nor the Supreme Court by more than six.[10]

The President's message recommending the measure dwelt on the complexities, delays and expense of litigation and the improbability that the ordinary private litigant could ever get the highest tribunal in the federal system to give him any hearing at all. Nothing was said about the fact that the addition of six new associate justices upon the supreme bench, besides perhaps aiding in the more speedy determination of cases, would also increase the probability that important cases would be decided in accordance with

9

the views of the executive. But notwithstanding the President's argument and in spite of what it omitted, the main purpose of the bill was in nowise obscured. Congressmen, newspapers, and the people immediately knew the issue for what it was. Political lines were drawn accordingly.

The President had been correct in expecting his measure to meet the approval of organized labor, still licking wounds received at the hands of the Supreme Court when the Railway Pension Act and the Guffey Coal Act were struck down, and in counting on support of politically-minded farmers smarting from their brush with the Court over the Agricultural Adjustment Act. If ever executive had reason to rely upon the effect of political prestige to re-enforce the strength of his argument, the President had that too. These things, being the master politician that he was, he had known from the beginning.

What apparently he did not know, or perhaps reckoned too lightly, was the public attachment to the doctrine that the Supreme Court, right or wrong, must remain beyond partisan manipulation. This manifestation of the American spirit is a peculiar phenomenon. No one loves the Supreme Court or its members in the sense that an executive or legislative leader is admired, applauded and followed. Not one citizen in a score can name the justices nor recognize them from their photographs. On a popular radio program called "Information Please" where a group of exceptionally well-informed persons submit themselves to a series of miscellaneous questions, a question that confounded the whole group in 1945 was one that called for the names of all members of the Supreme Court.

Nevertheless there is a deep current of feeling that somehow neither tyranny nor ill-considered experiment can do the country permanent damage as long as nine elderly men are permitted to function in their accustomed manner. It may be that this feeling is not very different in origin from that with which the English regard the crown. Few subjects consider that it matters much whether the king is good, bad or indifferent, but most are convinced that it matters a great deal that he exists, a reassuring sign that the country has not been swept away from its ancient moorings. Had the President consulted his Secretary of State about public attachment to the principle of judicial independence he might have been reminded that in the Secretary's native state a governor had been politically destroyed and compelled to retire from a contest for re-election because it was said that he had sought to influence a decision in a case pending in the state supreme court,[11] and that a similar sentiment could reasonably be expected at the national level.

Indications that the President had ordered more than Congress was willing to deliver were not long in multiplying. Not merely Republicans and conservative Democrats expressed objections, but many liberal Democrats spoke against or withheld approval of the President's plan. Uncertain members, instead of being pushed into accord with the policy of the President by public sentiment as had often happened before, were now pulled in the opposite direction by the same force, for an overwhelming majority of those who took it upon themselves to let their senators know their views spoke out in condemnation of the bill.

Throughout the spring of 1937 the "Court Fight" occupied

prime place in the public's political interest.[12] The coterie that stood by the President were at first loath to concede defeat, but one after another was convinced, and at length the President himself accepted the report of Vice-President Garner that there remained no choice for the passage of the measure even in modified form. The victory of his opponents was complete and in July the bill was re-committed to the judiciary committee with assurances from administration senators that when a new measure for judicial reform was reported it would not affect the Supreme Court.

One of the administration stalwarts who had enthusiastically supported the President's plan to enlarge the Court was Senator Hugo L. Black of Alabama. Throughout the six-months fight he had been generally regarded as among the comparatively few senators who supported the President's plan out of conviction, and such senators could not be so readily forgiven by the bill's enemies as those who had supported it only in response to White House pressure or party loyalty. It seemed pretty certain that Senator Black would be called upon to defend his position when time came for the voters of Alabama to elect his successor. His political prospects looked none too rosy.

The retirement of Justice Willis Van Devanter was expected to make room for the first Roosevelt appointment to the supreme bench and it was generally understood that Senator Joseph Robinson of Arkansas would be the President's choice. But Senator Robinson died suddenly and the President, upon the retirement of Justice Van Devanter in the summer of 1937, astonished the nation by appointing Senator Black.

12

Looking backward it can be seen that there were several reasons for this choice. Foremost was the need to appoint a senator, for the Senate was not in a tractable mood and the appointment of any man who was the kind of appointee that President Roosevelt wanted was certain to provoke a fight unless by the appointment of a senator advantage could be taken of the time-honored rule of senatorial courtesy which makes confirmation of a senator's nomination virtually a foregone conclusion. Senator Minton of Indiana was a possibility, but his attacks upon the Court during the fight over increasing its membership had so nearly approached the personal that he is said to have advised against his own appointment. Also Minton's obligation to the McNutt organization in Indiana was the kind of handicap from which Black was free, for he had risen to position in spite of machines, and had built his organization from the ground.

Sectionally, too, advantages were with Black. The South was not represented on the Court unless Justice McReynolds from the border state of Kentucky was considered Southern. The federal circuit from which Black hailed was extensive and the states which composed it needed some sort of salving from the hands of the President. Appointment there would leave the Court better balanced geographically than it had been for some time. Best of all, Black's course in the Senate gave the President sound reason to expect that he would be satisfactory as a judge. He appeared to be a liberal from conviction and from a region where all who followed the line of least resistance gravitated in the other direction.

Chess players have a name for that unfortunate position to

which a player is brought when, rather than make any possible move, he would prefer to allow his pieces to remain as they stand. His opponent, of course, delights in his predicament. It is altogether possible that President Roosevelt who played the game of politics with great relish and consummate skill enjoyed the prospect of seeing the conservatives of the Senate confronted with the alternatives of voting to confirm a pronounced New Dealer or deserting the rule of senatorial courtesy by which all senators set such store. While the President may have enjoyed the anticipation of the discomfiture of reactionary senators, he probably had little doubt as to their ultimate course.

On the sultry afternoon in mid-August when the President's messenger arrived at the doors of the Senate Chamber bearing a sealed envelop containing the announcement of his nominee to succeed Justice Van Devanter, neither the tired senators nor their newspaper reading constituents were prepared for what was about to happen. Once again the President had kept his plans a close secret. When Vice-President Garner announced the nomination of Senator Black, Senator Ashurst, staunch New Dealer and Chairman of the Judiciary Committee, promptly arose and moved immediate confirmation. The strategy did not work. The veteran Hiram Johnson objected to an executive session for immediate confirmation,[13] and from this time on it was obvious that there would be a fight by those who were unwilling to allow the elevation of Senator Black without at least registering their protest. Most were not so outspoken as Senator Carter Glass who when told that Black's appointment was a great victory for the common people, is said to have responded that "they must be God-damned

14

common" if Black's selection suited them,[14] but many harbored such views in silence or expressed them less emphatically.

Notwithstanding the advantage that any senator enjoys when the confirmation of his appointment comes before the body in which he sits, there were countervailing personal influences of no little importance. Republican toes had been stepped on frequently by the Senator from Alabama and his heavy heel was not easily forgot. Deep scars remained among the conservatives who had been the targets of his shafts, and many senators sincerely regarded him as too partisan and radical to be safely entrusted with judicial responsibility.

It was chiefly upon the conduct of two investigating committees he had headed, one on ocean and air mail subsidies and one on lobbying activities, that Senator Black's reputation rested. Through his vigor in this work he had won the right to be regarded as a worthy successor to Thomas J. Walsh who had conducted the Teapot Dome inquiry ten years earlier. It was conceded that his management of both investigations had been skillful, but many thought that his skill was no more than the ability of a practiced prosecuting attorney to sense the suspicious, entangle witnesses, and embarrass adversaries. Time and again his pitiless probing had reached the seats of admitted infection, but the opinion was widely held that he also enjoyed too much the task of tearing away the concealing tissues.

The paths of his investigations had been lurid with charges and countercharges, *subpoenas duces tecum,* searches and seizures, and contempt proceedings. Reluctant witnesses had ended up in jail, respectable reputations had fallen apart like decayed wood, and numerous stuffed shirts had been depleted of the straw which had given them such eminent appearances.[15] The ocean and air mail contracts had been awarded to political favorites, and Senator Black had exposed the methods employed in awarding them. Lobbying had become a stench in the nostrils of decent persons who had to watch what was going on, and the work of Black's committee pointed out the locations from which the most offensive odors were arising. But in accomplishing these ends he seemed to many to have little respect for either the requirements of polite conduct or the limitations of law.

In the investigation of the ocean and air mail contracts the reputation of President Hoover's Postmaster General was badly damaged, and although it was pretty obvious that in passing out million dollar favors he had concerned himself more with political merit than with public service, his friends felt that he was being made the whipping boy for a wrath that was both partisan and malignant. Former cabinet members in an administration even as politically discredited as Hoover's are not without influence. All lobbyists worth their salt have good friends among the legislators. Since lobbying is a two-way activity and a lobbyist must necessarily have someone to lobby with, the exposure of a lobbyist often strikes very close to a vulnerable spot in the body of gentlemen with whom he lobbies. Naturally when an investigation of lobbying begins there is a widespread scurrying to cover, but in the investigation conducted by Senator Black the lights had come on too suddenly for all to escape identification. The recognition of certain familiar faces caused no end of embarrassment.

Enemies made by the investigations Black had conducted now

rose to plague the inquisitor. The man who had ruthlessly torn off the garments of others was now about to run the gantlet where every hand would have the opportunity to snatch at his; the police officer who had given suspects the third degree under Kleig lights was now going to have to sit in their glare himself.

The immediate reaction of the press did nothing to discourage the conduct of the ordeal. From all parts of the country and from almost all shades of political color came condemnation of the President's appointment. For the frankly anti-Roosevelt press, the New York *Herald Tribune* uttered this fairly typical comment:

Not even those closest to the President on Capitol Hill dreamed that he would make the defiant gesture of nominating Senator Black to the Supreme Court . . . Senator Black's record at the bar offers not the slightest qualification for the high office to which the President would elevate him. His real qualification is plainly the intensity of his New Deal support. He is one of the few who stood by the Court packing plan to its grim death. . . . The meager technical equipment of Senator Black for one of the greatest judicial posts in the world makes his selection unsuitable. His subserviency to the New Deal gives a political cast to his candidacy which is highly unfortunate. Even more his service as chairman of the Senate Lobby Investigating Committee revealed such an utter lack of judicial spirit, such a complete scorn of constitutional restraints as would make his ascent to the Supreme Bench a national tragedy . . . the nomination is as menacing as it is unfit.[16]

The somewhat independent Washington *Post* was scarcely less critical and declared that,

Men deficient in the necessary qualifications have occasionally been named to the Supreme Court. And qualified men have been put forward because they are also agreeable to a president. But until yesterday students of American history would have found it difficult to refer to any Supreme Court nomination which combined lack of training on the one hand and

17

extreme partisanship on the other. In this one respect the choice of Senator Black must be called outstanding.[17]

In the appointee's home city the Birmingham *Age-Herald* reported that news of Senator Black's appointment had produced a great conflict of emotion and judgment, and for its own part announced:

We fear he may not prove the great judge. We think Mr. Roosevelt at this time of extreme feeling did no service to the judicial ideals of this country in appointing a man around whom so much of that feeling centers. But even so we hold to a faith in Hugo Black's fundamental sincerity and his broad mental character.[18]

Writing in the New York *Times* Arthur Krock remarked that the appointee was a man of no judicial experience and one in whom "watchers of his career have never discovered a trace of the judicial temperament."[19] He was said to be suspicious, intolerant, and careless of private rights. Always his conduct of the lobby investigation was cited to illustrate this last named fault.

To be sure the daily press was not unanimous in adverse criticism. The Philadelphia *Record* was of the opinion that the President had made a "great nomination of an outstanding liberal, a man of wide knowledge and acute understanding,"[20] but such favorable comment was almost exclusively from those who consistently supported whatever the President did, a segment of the press neither large nor influential. Occasionally some of those who regretted the appointment conceded that the appointee was not without his better qualities. Among these the correspondent of the New York *Times* took some hope from the fact that Black was "relentlessly intelligent, uninterested in acquiring money, deeply solicitous of the poor and oppressed (unless the oppressed are fighting his ideas), and sensitive to criticism."[21]

Among the weeklies the response was little better. Writing in *Newsweek,* Raymond Moley remarked that there might have been worse appointments to judicial office, but that he could not remember where nor when. This former friend of Roosevelt found in Black a close counterpart of Huey Long, although he could not credit Black with anything like the Louisianian's constructive achievement. "Black," said Moley, "looms only as a destroyer, an attacker, an inquisitioner," whose prominence as a national figure was the "product of that dark political hour in the Twenties when fiery crosses flared on thousands of hillsides." [22]

Black's early support from the Ku Klux Klan intruded even among comments most favorable to his appointment. Among the left-wing liberal publications, the *New Republic* expressed doubt as to whether the selection was a wise one,[23] and the *Nation,* which called his appointment the most encouraging since that of Brandeis, attempted to explain his Klan support as due to nothing more than his "Southern background." Once on the Supreme Court, it suggested, he would be able to "clear away the barnacles gathered from a political voyage in Southern waters."[24]

Vigorous objections were urged by the Catholic press. In one Catholic weekly review a Jesuit priest in an editorial entitled, "The Old Klan Vermin and the New Court Ermine,"[25] recalled that in 1921 Senator Black had successfully defended a man who had killed a Catholic priest and had been supported by the Ku Klux Klan in his race for the Senate. *Commonweal,* representing the liberal Catholic element, was more reserved but declared that "the faith and confidence of the American people in our democratic institutions has in no way been strengthened by this appointment."[26]

Negro opinion seemed more divided. The Baltimore *Afro-American,* typical of the chain of newspapers of similar names, asked if the President had so hypnotized Catholics, Jews, and colored people by his dynamic personality that they were " unconscious of the principles upon which Senator Black must stand."[27] However, from Black's own state came a telegram from the president of Tuskegee Institute, a leading Negro college, congratulating the appointee and wishing him well.[28]

Encouraged by this kind of reaction, senators who opposed the appointment girded themselves to block confirmation. Burke of Nebraska, Bridges of New Hampshire, and Copeland of New York appeared to form the spearhead of the attack. The judiciary committee of which Senator Black's friend, Senator Ashurst, was chairman, lost no time in returning a favorable report, but its session was said to have been a stormy one during the course of which Senator Neely of West Virginia left the room in a temper and Senators Dietrich and Burke almost came to blows. The final vote was 13 to 4 in favor of confirmation, two Democrats and two Republicans constituting the opposition.[29]

When the matter finally reached the Senate the first objection raised was a technical one. Senator White of Maine declared that no vacancy on the Court had resulted by reason of Justice Van Devanter's retirement, since a vacancy could occur only by those means mentioned in the Constitution: impeachment, resignation or death. Since there was no vacancy, he argued, Congress, by passing the retirement act providing for a new justice to replace the one who had retired, had created a new office, which Black, who had been a member of the creating Congress, could not constitutionally

20

accept.[30] With somewhat better reasoning he pointed out that by providing for retirement privileges Congress had increased the emoluments of the office of Supreme Court Justice and thereby had made all members of the present Congress ineligible to fill the place upon the Court.

Entering the debate at this turn, Senator Bridges of New Hampshire added a point to the argument against confirmation by charging that the judiciary committee which had reported favorably upon Black's nomination had taken its action without public hearings. He demanded that the committee reopen its hearings and offered to submit to it the names of a number of persons he wished to have called as witnesses. Of course, he added, he did not mean by such a demand any personal reflection upon Senator Black.

It was while his colleagues were thus disporting themselves in a sort of sham battle exercise, disclaiming each in turn any personal reflection upon the character of the nominee, that Senator Royal S. Copeland of New York fired into the ranks of the confirmationists a full round of the deadly ammunition that was to affect the Black reputation so adversely in the days ahead. As he saw the matter, the occasion called for the raw truth and the time had now come to discard the polite pretense of personal good feeling that had so far covered the debate. "Personally," he declared, "I feel so outraged by this proposal to put a Klan sympathizer upon the Bench that it is difficult to discuss the matter in temperate language,"[31] whereupon he launched into a violent tirade of denunciation of the Klan and the man who had become Senator by virtue of its support. To arouse Catholic hearers he pictured their churches destroyed and their priests massacred. For the Negroes he reviewed the Scottboro case and asked them to speculate upon what a Mr. Justice Black would do if another such case ever came before the Court.

Next Senator Burke discussed Black's membership in the Klan and asserted that he had talked with a gentleman who had been present when Black was initiated into the hooded order. This witness, he said, could be brought before the committee if further opportunity were given. Replying to Burke, Senator Borah, who was also on record as opposed to confirmation, declared that there had never at any time been "one iota of evidence that Senator Black was a member of the Klan," and that during the hearings no one " had suggested any source from which such evidence could be gathered."[32]

Senator Ashurst closed the debate with his typical irony, taking note of how some of the same people who professed to object to Black upon suspicion that he was a Klansman had likewise complained against the nomination of Justice Cardozo because he was a Jew. Upon the final vote 63 senators voted for confirmation and 16 opposed it. Senator Black was now entitled to take the oath and enter upon his duties as an Associate Justice of the Supreme Court of the United States.

CHAPTER II

" I DID JOIN THE KLAN "

It was well for Black that the Senate fight ended when it did and that the judiciary committee had not reopened hearings on his nomination, for within a few days news articles began to appear that might well have prevented confirmation had they been published beforehand. No sooner had Black been sworn in and set sail for Europe for an interim vacation than the Ku Klux issue bobbed up again, supported this time by what purported to be authenticated documents.

Whether the revelation owed its origin to a New York private detective as some reported, or as others supposed to a disgruntled member of the Klan who resented Black's departure from the principles of that organization, or to some other source, the conduit through which it reached the public was a series of copyrighted articles in the Pittsburgh *Post-Gazette,* a newspaper published by Paul Block whom the Nation termed, "a Hearst stooge,"[1] and which were also circulated by the American Newspaper Alliance.

The first article asserted that Justice Black had become a part of the Invisible Empire by joining Robert E. Lee Klan Number 1 on September 11, 1923; that he resigned on July 9, 1925, on the eve of his campaign for the United States Senate; and that after his nomination in the Democratic primary he had been welcomed back into the fold at a state Kloreo held in Birmingham on September 2, 1926, at which time he had been made a life member. These statements were said to be based on the official records of the Klan meetings and a copy of Senator Black's resignation found in the organization's files. This purported resignation read:

July 9, 1925

Mr. J. W. Hamilton, Kligraph
Birmingham, Alabama

Dear Sir and Klansman:

Beg to tender you herewith my resignation as a member of the Ku Klux Klan effective from this date on.

Yours I. T. S. U. B.

Hugo L. Black

The letters I. T. S. U. B. were said to signify "in the sacred unfailing bond."

According to the writer of this article, the resignation had been for campaign purposes only and was merely placed in the Klan files and never acted upon. After the nomination had been won, he continued, Black made a speech in which he attributed his victory to Klan support saying, "I realize that I was elected by men who believe in the principles I have sought to advocate and which are the principles of this organization."[2] It was on this occasion that Black was supposed to have received a life membership card which entitled him still to enter the Klan Klaverns and participate in Klan Kloreos.

Arthur Krock, correspondent of the New York *Times* and not generally given to the repetition of mere gossip, reported that President Roosevelt was "deeply perturbed" by the turn affairs had taken and by the news that his new appointee was actually a mem-

24

ber of the Klan. "It is not in the least surprising," wrote this observer,

to hear reliably that the President is both politically and personally upset by the charges made against Justice Black. . . . Even if it should be demonstrated that Mr. Black is no longer a Klansman, but once was, the President will be left in the position of having, on a vengeful impulse, elevated to the administration of highest justice one who subscribed to an intolerance against which he has fought all of his life.[3]

The President, for his part, made no comment but this:

I know only what I have read in the newspapers. I note that the stories are running serially, and their publication is not complete. Mr. Justice Black is in Europe where undoubtedly he cannot get the full text of these articles. Until such time as he returns, there is no further comment to be made.[4]

That there was further comment to be made, however, even if not by President Roosevelt, was increasingly evident. Day by day newspaper editorials, organization resolutions, and public statements by politicians accumulated. The National Association for the Advancement of Colored People urged the President to call upon his appointee to resign unless he could disprove that he had been a member of the Klan. The Catholic Club of the City of New York unanimously adopted resolutions demanding that he resign from the Court or else be impeached unless full and satisfactory evidence should promptly prove the falsity of such charges. The American Bar Association through its general assembly declined to make a direct investigation of the new Justice but the move for such an investigation was defeated by a majority of but 22 votes out of 354. When the fight was resumed at the general session of the Bar Association the matter was apparently compromised by the adoption of a resolution petitioning the Senate to hold public hearings on all judicial appointments in the future.

In the meantime from Justice Black in Europe there came no comment. While he was in Paris and London reporters had been unable to locate him, let alone get an interview. As his ship plowed through Hampton Roads, however, a full hundred of them were accorded an opportunity to welcome him to his native shores in typical American fashion. After pictures had been taken from all angles the reporters squared themselves for the promised interview. "Make it short and snappy," said the quarry. "What are your immediate plans?" was the first question, and by the time the reply that he was going to Washington had been made, someone remarked, "And now for the burning question." The Justice did not wait for the question to be further defined. "When I have any statement to make that is definite or final on any subject, I will make it in such a way that I cannot be misquoted," he said, "and that the nation can hear me."[5]

Then to make it plain that he wanted no one connected with the press to miss the implication, he continued,

If I make any statement it will be in a way the people can hear me and understand what I have to say, and not have to depend on some parts of the press which might fail to report all I have to say. It will be no use to ask me anything else.[6]

In the face of this declaration a reporter from the New York *Times* persisted, "Will you answer the specific question whether you are or have ever been a member of the Invisible Empire, Knights of the Ku Klux Klan?" The reply was a repetition of what the new Justice had just said about his distrust of parts of the press. When another reporter offered to show him copies of the *Post-Gazette* containing the Sprigle stories he curtly answered, "You can take them back to Mr. Block."[7] This interview, of course, did nothing to improve the new Justice's press relations. *Editor and Publisher* termed his remarks "in execrable taste," and thought they did not at all illustrate "the judicial temperament associated with the Supreme Bench."[8]

Notwithstanding Justice Black's refusal to satisfy the demands of the reporters who had besieged him at Norfolk, the country did not have long to wait for his answer to "the burning question." Two days after his arrival in the United States he broadcast this speech by radio:

Ladies and Gentlemen:

The Constitution is the Supreme Law of our Country. The Bill of Rights is the heart of the Constitution.

The Constitutional safeguard to complete liberty of religious belief is a declaration of the greatest importance to the future of America as a nation of free people. Any movement or action by any group that threatens to bring about a result inconsistent with this unrestricted individual right is a menace to freedom.

Let me repeat:

Any program, even if directed by good intention, which tends to breed or revive religious discord or antagonism can and may spread with such rapidity as to imperil this vital constitutional protection of one of the most sacred of human rights.

I believe that no ordinary maneuver executed for political advantage would justify a member of the Supreme Court in publicly discussing it. If, however, that maneuver threatens the existing peace and harmony between religious or racial groups in our country, the occasion is not an ordinary one. It is extraordinary.

During my recent absence on a short vacation abroad, a planned and concerted campaign was begun which fans the flames of prejudice and

27

is calculated to create racial and religious hatred. If continued, the inevitable result will be the projection of religious beliefs into a position of prime importance in political campaigns and to reinfect our social and business life with the poison of religious bigotry.

It will bring the political religionist back into undeserved and perilous influence in the affairs of government. It will elevate the least worthy to political positions because religion or race bars others from a password. It will resurrect practices and arguments from which this country suffered sorely in the nineteen-twenties. It will revive the spirit which in 1928 caused a national campaign to be waged largely upon issues unworthy of a free people.

It will bankrupt many business men whose sole offense is that they have religious beliefs which do not accord with the prevailing religion in their communities. It will punish the professional man whose patients and clients boycott him, not because of lack of professional ability, but because there are in his locality few members of his faith or race. It will set neighbor against neighbor and turn old friends into new enemies.

To contribute my part in averting such a catastrophe in this land dedicated to tolerance and freedom, I break with precedents of the past to talk with you tonight.

An effort is being made to convince the people of America that I am intolerant, and that I am prejudiced against people of the Jewish and Catholic faiths, and against members of the Negro race. These insinuations are advanced despite the fact that for the last eleven years, I have served in the Senate of the United States under constant and microscopic public scrutiny.

My words and acts are a matter of public record. I believe that my record as a Senator refutes every implication of racial and religious intolerance. It shows that I was of that group of liberal Senators who have consistently fought for the civil, economic and religious rights of all Americans without regard to race or creed.

The insinuations of racial and religious intolerance made concerning me are based on the fact that I joined the Ku Klux Klan about fifteen years ago. I did join the Klan. I later resigned. I never rejoined. What appeared then, or what appears now on the records of the organization, I do not know.

I have never considered and I do not now consider the unsolicited card given to me shortly after my nomination to the Senate as a membership of any kind in the Ku Klux Klan. I never used it. I did not even keep it.

Before becoming a Senator I dropped the Klan. I have had nothing whatever to do with it since that time. I abandoned it. I completely discontinued any association with the organization. I have never resumed it and never expect to do so.

At no meeting of any organization, social, political or fraternal, have I ever indicated the slightest departure from my steadfast faith in the unfettered right of every American to follow his conscience in matters of religion. I have no sympathy with any organization or group which, anywhere or at any time, arrogates to itself the un-American power to interfere in the slightest degree with complete religious freedom.

No words have ever been or will ever be spoken by me, directly or indirectly, indicating that any native or foreign born person in our free country should or could be restricted in his right to worship according to the dictates of his conscience. I have supported candidates for public office without regard to their faith. In my endorsement of applicants for governmental positions I have acted without discrimination of any kind or character.

I have among my friends many members of the colored race. I have watched the progress of its members with sympathy and admiration. Certainly they are entitled to the full measure of protection accorded to the citizenship of our country by the Constitution and our laws.

Some of my best and most intimate friends are Catholics and Jews. Shortly after I moved to Birmingham more than a quarter of a century ago, I formed one of the most valued friendships of my life with a son of Jewish faith. He was one of my closest associates and strongest political supporters. Months of our lives were spent together, much of the time in his home. He stood so nearly in the place of a father to me that while in the army in 1918 I designated this trusted Jewish friend as sole executor of my will. In my campaigns for public office his counsel and assistance were always mine. His widow, who was a guest in my home at the recent inauguration of President Roosevelt, was one of the first to congratulate me upon my nomination to be a Justice of the Supreme Court.

When this statement is ended my discussion of the question is closed.

I believe the character and conduct of every public servant, great and small, should be subject to the constant scrutiny of the people. This must be true if a democracy serves its purpose. It is in this spirit that I now bid those who have been listening to me good-night.[9]

Justice Black must be too astute a politician to have expected a favorable press reaction to his speech. Nothing would have brought about this result except an outright denial that he had ever taken the Klan's oath or donned its regalia. Since that could not be said, the situation resolved itself into an occasion when the best had to be made of a bad bargain for there was no escape from the necessity of making public answer to his accusers. The only open question so far as the reaction to be expected from the press was concerned was how violent it would be and how long it would continue. It turned out to be rather violent and it lasted a considerable while.

The New York *Herald Tribune* seemed to set the pace for the anti-Roosevelt papers. It declared that the Justice's whole conduct since the charges of Klan membership had been brought against him had been that of a " coward." It accused him of " skulking, dodging and running away," and finally "in a uniquely brazen utterance" adding "the vice of hypocrisy to his record of evasion."[10] In a lugubrious editorial the independent New York *Times* lamented "that a man who has ever taken the oath of allegiance to a sinister and destructive organization should now take his place on the highest court of justice in this country." The nomination it reiterated, was a "tragic blunder," resulting in the unfortunate condition that

at every session of the Court the presence on the bench of a Justice who has worn the white robe of the Ku Klux Klan will stand as a living symbol of the fact that here the cause of liberalism was unwittingly betrayed.[11]

The Democratic Boston *Post* called for Black's resignation, saying:

One who associates with bigots, bids for their support, takes the bigot's oath, and then is so craven that he allows his friends in a crisis to deny it all, can't clear himself by asserting that it was all contrary to his real character.[12]

The New Haven *Journal Courier* asserted that "the sensitive will avert their eyes,"[13] and the Washington *Post* considered that by this appointment the reputation of the American judiciary had been "permanently smirched."[14] The Albany *Knickerbocker News* thought that Justice Black's belated speech had sprinkled "another shower of soot upon the already discolored ermine of his new robes,"[15] and the Cleveland *News* declared his presence on the Court "a never ending insult to American ideals of government and American ideals of manhood."[16]

The Chicago *Tribune* called attention to the fact that even in his public statement he had not once condemned Klan or Klansmen,[17] and the Chattanooga *Times,* published in a city where Klan strength had once appeared to hold the balance of power between the party organizations, compared his statement to that of a "police court lawyer trying to obtain the dismissal of charges against a house-breaker by pleading that the defendant had always been kind to his family."[18]

Comment in the deep South was more apologetic than proud. The Columbia (South Carolina) *Record* hoped that "it may indeed happen that as a burnt child who dreads the fire he may turn out to be a champion of the Bill of Rights,"[19] and the Dallas *News* thought that although under the circumstances his defense had been fairly able, it was still true that he had joined the Ku Klux

Klan when forty years old and that it must be presumed that he knew at least some of its objectives.[20]

The situation was a natural for cartoonists. The New York *Sun* in a three column cut published a formal photograph of the Court with a hooded figure painted in over the picture of the retired Justice Van Devanter with the caption, "A Klansman Komes to Kourt."[21] In a cartoon entitled, "A Banner with a Strange Device," the Washington *Post* pictured a hooded klansman lifting high a sign reading, "An effort is being made to convince the people of America that I am intolerant,"[22] and in sections of Washington handbills were distributed calling October 4 "Black Day" to be mourned by the American people.

Among the magazines the appointment of the new Justice found an apologist in the *New Republic* and an outright defender in the *Nation.* The former remarked that while "both the Justice and the President have cut a sorry figure in this affair," it could be said in defense of membership in the Klan that joining it in Alabama in the early nineteen-twenties was much like joining the Rotary or Kiwanis Club in some small Midwestern town, and that along with Mr. Black, "there were thousands of middle-class people who took the Klan oath without realizing the full significance of the hooded order or the hateful character of its doctrines." It suggested that the new Justice was perhaps "not a Klansman but simply a politician."[23]

The *Nation* was the periodical that took prime place among Justice Black's defenders, insisting that the tories were fighting Black not because of their horror at his affiliation with the Ku Klux Klan, but because of his liberal legislative record.

Admit that Black's connection with the Klan was unfortunate; admit that his silence under attack was a mistake, but do not be taken in by the attack itself. Look straight through it to the men who launched it, recognize them for the enemies of progress that they are, distinguish the hatred of Roosevelt and his progressive legislation that animated them, examine the legislative record of the man chosen as their victim; and then decide whether Hugo Black or Paul Block is closer to the spirit of the Ku Klux Klan.[24]

The most vituperative periodical was the *American Mercury.* In an article by Albert Nock it accused President Roosevelt of making the appointment "in a fit of swaggering bad temper." Justice Black was characterized as "a vulgar dog who rifles other people's correspondence," and was said to be totally incapable of writing judicial opinions. "Everyone concerned in these misfeasances," concluded Mr. Nock, "has indelibly marked himself contemptible."[25]

Among the groups supposed to have been the objects of Ku Klux Klan antagonism the Jews seemed to show the most tolerant spirit toward the past affiliations of Justice Black. The *Jewish Times* of Baltimore was somewhat typical in expressing itself as preferring to believe that Justice Black's interest in the Klan "was no more than his desire to get votes in a state in which the Klan was then a dominant figure."[26] In other words, it thought that Black's membership in the Klan might be excused on the ground that he was using it merely to sell the people of Alabama a bill of goods. To be sure the Jewish papers did not applaud the appointment but the acrimony that characterized the Catholic and Negro press was lacking. Possibly Black's efforts to expose the purposes behind the anti-Semitic Sentinels of the Republic had some influence in this direction.

The *Catholic World* in a sarcastic article analyzed Justice Black's speech paragraph by paragraph, ending each with, "So Mr. Black joined the Ku Klux Klan." It also suggested that the whole affair be made into a musical comedy in which the ghosts of John Marshall and Roger B. Taney should appear, their faces crimson at the shame that had been brought upon the Court, and in which Mr. Black should sing the following ditty:

> I hate religious prejudice, and so I joined the Klan.
> I love my friends, the Catholics, and so I joined the Klan.
> Izzy and Ikey are pals of mine, and so I joined the Klan.

But in the end the writer dropped his levity and concluded, "It is no joke. It is a first class calamity."[27]

Such was the reaction of the American press and American politicians to the appointment and its aftermath. By the end of 1937 many more people than usually concern themselves with judicial appointment knew the arguments pro and con provoked by the selection of Senator Black. After Black's membership in the Klan was made public, but before his radio address, the American Institute of Public Opinion ran a poll containing the following questions:

When President Roosevelt appointed Senator Black to the Supreme Court did you approve the appointment?

If a man has been a member of the Ku Klux Klan should this bar him from serving as a Supreme Court Judge?

Should Justice Black resign from the Supreme Court if it is proved that he has been a member of the Ku Klux Klan?

To the first question 56 per cent of those polled answered that they had favored Black when he was first appointed. To the second question 57 per cent replied, yes, and to the third question 55 per cent answered, yes. Sentiment against Black, according to this poll, was strongest on the Pacific Coast, but almost as strong in New England and the Middle Atlantic States. Only in the South did a majority hold that he should retain his seat.[28]

By October 24 the same poll reported that the demand for the Justice's resignation had dropped sharply. Whether this was due to the lapse of time during which tempers had time to cool or to the effect of Black's radio broadcast is a matter of conjecture, but now only 44 per cent of those addressed thought he should resign. To the question whether Congress should impeach Justice Black only 31 per cent answered, yes.[29]

In its January 1938 issue, *Fortune* reported that after "most of the sound and fury had died down and Justice Black had graduated from the front pages to the hushed silences of the Supreme Court Chambers," it had taken a poll upon the question whether the choice of Justice Black had been a good or a bad one. The poll had shown these results:

	Total	Northeast	Southeast	Prosperous	Poor
Good Choice	22%	15.6%	32.5%	15.5%	25.5%
Fair Choice	12.8	8.4	13.5	11.7	11.8
Bad Choice	36.2	48.4	23.7	58.6	25.3
Don't Know	29	27.6	30.3	14.2	37.4

From these figures *Fortune* concluded that four months after the appointment the new Justice did not appear "to be the object of any great national indignation," although more people regarded his appointment as bad than good. Of those who thought the appointment bad, 48 per cent objected on the grounds of his Klan membership, 24 per cent because of his lack of judicial experience, 17 per cent on the ground that it was a political appointment, and the remainder did not approve the choice, but did not know why they objected to it.[30] How accurate a reflection of sentiment such a poll may be is a question that permits much difference of opinion, but it may be accepted as fairly indicating a current lack of confidence among a large part of the population.

One last hurdle remained for Justice Black to clear and it proved to be a minor one. Two Boston lawyers, one a former assistant attorney-general, undertook to have the Supreme Court deny him his seat on the ground that having been a member of the Congress that increased the emoluments of the office of Supreme Court Justice, he was ineligible for the appointment. On the very day on which Justice Black ascended the Supreme Court bench for the first time the Chief Justice read a *per curiam* opinion making short work of the matter on the ground that the petitioners lacked sufficient legal interest in the question raised to entitle them to a hearing.[31]

It was in this atmosphere that the new Justice assumed his duties and set about preparing his first sheaf of opinions.

CHAPTER III

THE SENATOR FROM ALABAMA

When Justice Black's political career is reviewed it becomes apparent that neither the material nor the mold was such as to commend him to conservative Americans with the conventional ideas of what it takes to make an acceptable Supreme Court member. Born in Clay County, Alabama, the son of a combination country storekeeper and farmer, he had grown to maturity in a region of political paradox. The county of his birth lies between the hill country of the north and the so-called "black belt" and in characteristics more nearly resembles the former. While it would not produce a town like Cullman, so dominated by hill-dwellers' antipathies that for many years a sign was displayed warning Negroes not to remain over night, it was even less like the magnolia-scented countryside around Montgomery where economy is still geared to the plantation system.

Since an able-minded "poor boy"[1] with a talent for forensics and a strong personal ambition has often gone far along the road to political preferment, there is nothing very unusual in the fact that Hugo Black should push his way through the law school of the University of Alabama to attain professional and political prominence. Neither is it uncommon for such a one, if he enters politics, consciously to direct his appeal to that portion of the population that enjoys least under the existing order. Talmadges, Longs, and Bilbos bear witness to the possibility of success by this route.

Hugo Black, however, differed from the conventional type in that his urge to improve the poor man's lot did not in any wise abate when he had accomplished his personal quest for office. On the contrary, his views progressively developed in the same fixed direction and each forward step in his thinking appeared to reinforce his conviction that the ills of the people demanded radical remedies. Even in his circles of confidence he kept insisting that there was something more than buncombe in the vote-getting slogans invented for use upon the hustings.

By the time Hugo Black had reached his twenty-first birthday it was apparent that he had surveyed the prospects of popularity and calculated the means of obtaining it. Masonic mummery, secret society ceremonials, civic club displays of fellowship, and political barbecues exerted an attraction hardly to be explained by a mere desire to mix with his fellow beings for the sake of their company. The first reward for his active participation in such activities came when at the age of twenty-four he became a Birmingham police judge.

While the police bench in Birmingham cannot be said to be much of a law school, it is an excellent academy for a study of some of the South's social problems. Birmingham in 1910 was a manufacturing city of 132,000 of whom 52,000 were Negroes. Its residents liked to call it the "Magic City" because of its rapid growth which was due to the dual proximity of coal and iron. It regularly competed for the doubtful honors of holding the nation's highest homicide and syphilis rate.

The pitiable array of unfortunates that daily parades before a police judge must soon convince him of the futility of attempting to cope with the problem of petty crime by any method of individual reform. On the other hand, the similarity of the incidents presented tends to encourage a hope of finding some method whereby society may prevent what it cannot cure and by which the cause of social maladjustment rather than its result may become the focus of corrective effort. One has only to concede that Hugo Black at the age of twenty-four was a young man of normal humane instincts and common intelligence to be certain that the experience of this period of his life furnished a basis for the framework of his maturer views. He early came to the conclusion that criminals were generally not made by some inherent strain of vicious propensity but by poverty and its attendant frustrations.

There remain accounts of incidents occurring during his police court days which were later used as evidence of his warm humanity. One such example is that of a Negro furnace worker haled into court for assaulting a white furniture dealer who was attempting to claim some second-hand furniture. When the judge heard testimony that the purchaser had already paid $94 in installments on $50 worth of household goods which, in default of further payment, were about to be removed from the bedroom of the defendant's sick wife, his wrath broke loose and besides dismissing the assault case he threatened the furniture dealer with a jail term if he ever molested the Negro again.[2]

It came as naturally as a weather change for the young police judge to aspire to become Jefferson County's prosecuting attorney, an office which is often a stepping stone to further political power. On first thought one might surmise that the duty of publicly denouncing one's fellow citizens before juries in an effort to send them to jail would not make for popularity, but experience shows that public prosecutors in the United States easily find means to compensate for this disadvantage. Law-abiding citizens are inclined to regard prosecuting attorneys as wholesome scourges for the unruly, while that element of the population that lives upon the borderline of legality, or perhaps just beyond it, has abundant incentive to keep in the good graces of the official who can suggest *nolle prosequis* and light sentences. Likewise it is to be considered that folks who go to prison are usually without many influential friends, while many who deserve to go but do not are able aides on election day. So Judge Black's discerning judgment pointed to the prosecuting attorney's office as the next step in his career, and his police connections and wide assortment of acquaintances enabled him to take it. In 1915 he was elected to this position.

Birmingham's recollection of Hugo Black's tenure as prosecuting attorney reflects favorably upon his character and capacity. It is generally agreed that he was able and vigorous, but neither unfair nor inconsiderate. Besides furnishing a step to political advancement the office he held offered an opportunity for experience in rough and tumble trial practice not to be found elsewhere. That Black was an apt student in the courses his new law school had to offer was soon apparent and what he learned there has often been evidenced in his later life. His term of office was cut short by the declaration of war, and in 1917 he joined the army, enrolled in an officer's candidate school, and emerged as a Captain in the Field Artillery.

Returning to Alabama at the end of the war he entered private practice and opened a law office with his brother in Birmingham.

The reputation of the firm was soon extensive and the returns remunerative. Martindale's *Legal Directory* for the year 1925 accorded Black the highest rating for both character and legal ability. His training and inclination well fitted him to be a plaintiff's lawyer, and it was soon recognized that in personal damage suits a litigant could not do better in the selection of counsel. He likewise became well known in the ranks of organized labor and successfully represented several large unions. In his first race for the Senate an opponent was to refer to him as "just another damage suit lawyer," but this denomination does the scope and character of his practice an injustice. The firm of Black and Black was concerned in almost every field of litigation and was well known throughout the state.

The son of the country storekeeper had now attained distinction in his profession but he could not forget his early taste for politics, and when Senator Oscar Underwood made public his decision to retire in 1926 Black immediately announced that he would be a candidate for his seat. The opposition he faced in his first campaign might well have daunted a young man of less determination and ambition. There were four other candidates, each with some reputation in conducting political contests. Thomas E. Kilby was a former governor and a man of considerable means; L. Breckinridge Musgrove was a millionaire coal operator with wide business connections and an organization and acquaintanceship which he had built up in two races against Oscar Underwood; John H. Bankhead was a member of the most eminent political family in Alabama; and James J. Mayfield was a retired Justice of the State Supreme Court and an able constitutional lawyer.

Against this field of opponents Black began a county by county campaign that required thirteen months and carried him into every county in the state and into some of them several times. Driving a Model T Ford from hamlet to hamlet he proved himself an able and indefatigable campaigner. Repeatedly claiming the distinction of being the only man of the people and son of toil in the contest, he attracted the support of organized labor, small farmers and— the Ku Klux Klan.

The Ku Klux Klan in the nineteen-twenties was one of those manifestations of growing pains that have occasionally occurred in American history when native sons begin to suspect that their ancient dominance is threatened by some group of upstarts who live and act in ways that are strange and foreign. It adopted the nomenclature, regalia, and some of the practices of the secret brotherhood that shortly after the War Between the States had sought by terrorism to prevent the lately freed Negroes and their allies from taking over the governments of the reconstructed states. By the middle nineteen-twenties it had risen to heights of political power not scaled before by any secret order in the United States. Appealing to racial and religious prejudice, posing as the protector of the moral code and the vindicator of righteousness, furnishing an opportunity for mystic ritualism, clandestine politics and occasional spasms of mob violence, the new society made marvelous headway. Particularly strong in the South and the Middlewest, it finally found itself able to name governors and negotiate with politicians high and low for the favor of its support.

It is likely that the great majority of Klansmen did not join because of any malicious or vindictive inclinations. Many joined because they were flattered that they did not have to remain outside the secret sessions where the "better element" was planning to outwit the undesirables, many joined to find a social outlet, and still others of a more practical nature because of business, professional, or political advantages. It is said that salesmen who lacked knowledge of the secret handclasp found themselves unable to sell a bill of goods in numerous Klan-ridden communities, and it is not surprising that they joined with little serious thought and less compunction. Hugo Black, political salesman that he was, was probably among the group that joined for a very practical purpose. Certainly he had never evinced any racial or religious bigotry and it is hardly likely that he expected to reform the country by wearing a mask or erecting fiery crosses.

As the 1926 senatorial race took shape in Alabama, it became evident that Black was the choice of a majority of local Klansmen although the national organization had promised Klan support to Colonel Musgrove. It may be that the Alabama Klan's support of Black was a reaction against the effort to control its course from national headquarters, but whatever the cause, it was soon conceded that the Alabama Klan was backing Black's candidacy. In the final count Black won by a substantial plurality, leading his nearest opponent, John Bankhead, by 20,000 votes.

When Alabama's new senator arrived in the Republican-dominated Senate of 1927 he was the sole Democrat serving a first term. The only noteworthy fact about him seemed to be that he had won his seat by virtue of Klan support, and most senators regretfully expected to find in Black another provincial Southerner who would fall in line behind the Heflins, Smiths, and Bilbos. It was soon observed, however, that the junior Senator from Alabama was not what had been expected. He had never served in a legislative body and was unfamiliar with legislative procedure but he knew enough to keep quiet until he had mastered parliamentary practice. During this period of his quiescence he began to be regarded as an affable gentleman, but was misappraised as a political nonentity. This inactive period of the Senator's career, however, did not last long. At first he became vocal as a mere objector and in this capacity was an annoying and persistent scourge of the Hoover administration. Also his tongue grew sharper in debate and those who felt his shafts had good reason to remember them.

Perhaps his prime interest at this stage of his career was in the public ownership of electric utilities. Soon after his arrival in the Senate he affiliated himself with Senator Norris and the group that was demanding the development of the government project at Muscle Shoals upon the Tennessee River. During the First World War the government had spent millions damming the river for the production of nitrates, only to stop the project when partially completed at the close of the war. In this condition it had remained for a decade, a monument pointed to by both the opponents of government operation of utilities and by those who favored the experiment. The former used it as an exhibit to prove how impractical it was to expect anything but waste and loss from government meddling in power production, while the latter contended that its uncompleted condition was evidence of what a stranglehold the private power companies had on a reactionary

Congress. The fact that the Alamaba Power Company and its confederates, which were naturally opposed to further development of the project, were strongly entrenched in Alabama politics did not deter Black from his course which he followed with dogged persistence.

Immediately after the stock market crash of 1929 the Hoover administration, alarmed—but not alarmed half enough—urged a legislative program the first item of which was a tax cut of some one hundred and sixty million dollars. Many Democrats hastened to announce their support of the administration's effort to bring about a tax cut, and Democratic Senators Harrison and Simmons publicly urged members of their party to fall in line with the suggestion of the Republicans and put aside further consideration of the pending tariff bill which was then being debated until a tax reduction resolution could be passed. Since unanimous consent was necessary to change the order of business to allow the passage of the tax measure any senator had it within his power to block the proposal. Such an opportunity did not escape Senator Black who announced that he had no notion of agreeing to change the order of business. For his part, he said, he thought it most important that the Senate should fix a date to consider a bill for the development at Muscle Shoals, and if debate on the tariff bill was going to be pushed aside for anything, it ought to be for this. It seemed that Senator Black could be quite as stubborn as some of his Southern colleagues who were more spectacular and picturesque. Likewise when President Hoover indicated his purpose to submit the World Court protocol to the Senate, Black as a member of the Foreign Relations Committee, opposed action upon the matter until after Muscle Shoals and other domestic issues should be considered.

As matters went from bad to worse for the Republican administration, the gad-fly activities of Senator Black increased. He denounced the action of the President in attempting to withhold from the Senate secret documents bearing on the London Naval Treaty; he criticized his plan to suspend for a year payments upon war debts; and he seized upon every opportunity to point out that the plight of the Hoover administration was but the culmination of Republican mismanagement beginning with the period of Harding normalcy.

In his second campaign for the Senate Black's political cunning was even more apparent than before. Throughout the country prohibition was a major issue and even in Alabama sentiment was rising to call for a review of the whole prohibition program. In this state of affairs Black again faced his old political enemy, ex-Governor Kilby, who was running on a wet platform. Of the other three candidates only one was a pronounced and unqualified dry. Senator Black managed to avoid commitment upon the prohibition issue and when the returns were in it was found that he had received 92,840 votes out of the total of 188,140 cast. The Alabama primary law had been altered after Black's race in 1926 and now required a majority for nomination instead of a plurality. Since Black's plurality was less than 700 votes short of a majority, his followers called upon Kilby to withdraw from the race in the interest of economy and party harmony. This Kilby refused to do, hoping no doubt to gain the support of those who had first cast their votes for the other wet candidates as well as to discredit Black with the drys.

No longer able to evade the prohibition issue, Black now declared in favor of a referendum, insisting that his own belief in prohibition had not changed, but that his devotion to democratic principle constrained him to favor an opportunity for popular expression. Although this could not have pleased the prohibitionists, they now had nowhere else to go except into the camp of a candidate avowedly wet. Black had managed to maintain his silence until a time when breaking it could not hurt him. His strategy was successful and in the run-off election he defeated Kilby by a comfortable majority.

Back in Washington Black found a new political climate. For the first time in his congressional career he was in company with a friendly administration and as Senior Senator from Alabama with six years of legislative experience behind him, he embarked upon a program of radical economic reform. The heart of this program was a bill to limit hours of labor to thirty per week and thus to spread more widely what jobs there were. This, he considered an almost sure cure for the country's vast unemployment problem.

Armed with a stupendous mass of statistics on unemployment, income, and production, Black argued loud and long for the adoption of his measure. Long hours and low wages, he insisted, lowered the level of production, retarded the improvement and expansion in the use of tools and machinery of output, closed factories, caused the abandonment of mines, paralyzed business, and brought destitution and suffering to helpless millions. Denying the common assertion of the period that the economic plight of the nation was the result of over-production, he pointed out that the country had never at any time produced enough consumer goods to supply the wants of all the people. The actual difficulty, he insisted, was not that too much was produced, but that the public was financially unable to buy what was produced and needed. His proposal, he declared, would put six million men back to work because producers, in order to keep their production up to the then prevailing level, would have to hire 25 per cent more workers who would then become potential customers and in turn stimulate further production.[3] Critics of the proposal pointed to the probability that the adoption of a thirty-hour week would result in a further lowering of wages or a sharp increase in the price of consumer goods. Further they reminded the proponents of the measure that to pass it would be but a futile gesture since it would be surely struck down by the Supreme Court.

Senator Black was already a favorite of organized labor, and his depression remedy further endeared him to this element. President William Green of the American Federation of Labor declared that the Black Bill was "the first constructive measure dealing with unemployment"[4] because it struck at the root of the problem resulting from technological progress.

Urged on by the labor lobby and by the insistence and persistence of Senator Black, the Senate in April 1933 passed his bill, but while it was pending in the House the administration's National Industrial Recovery bill came before Congress and was rapidly pushed through both chambers, superseding Senator Black's proposal. Black did not approve of the National Industrial Recovery Act and his loyalty to the Roosevelt administration did not deter him from saying so. He thought it fostered monopoly and would invite a multiplicity of difficulties through price fixing and wage regulation.

Senator Black devoted himself assiduously to the cause of social security. Declaring that a system of social security was not intended to destroy wealth but to use it,[5] he urged upon the Roosevelt administration a more radical and comprehensive program than it was undertaking. He disapproved the administration's policy of levying a tax on employees to help finance the unemployment compensation plan and suggested as a substitute an excess profits tax. In 1935 he introduced a health insurance bill under which the majority of persons earning less than $3,000 per year would receive essential medical services free.

To his legislative record, that had done anything but endear him to the conservatives, Senator Black in 1937 added a final chapter that convinced them that he was a dangerous enemy of the American system of government. He became one of the staunchest supporters of President Roosevelt's plan to enlarge the Supreme Court. As early as 1935 he had introduced a bill to speed up cases involving tests of federal statutes before the Supreme Court, under the provisions of which the Court would have been required to give such matters "preferential consideration over all other causes not of a like nature."[6] Chief Justice Hughes and Justices Van Devanter and Brandeis had appeared at the hearing and spoken in opposition to this proposal. When the Court declared the Agricultural Adjustment Act unconstitutional[7] Black gave out a statement to the press in which he said, "This means that 120,000,000 are ruled by five men,"[8] so it did not come as a surprise to the public to learn that he had declared himself in favor of the President's plan to reform the Court by enlarging it. Nor was Black content merely to go on record as favoring the proposal but became one of its active proponents. In a radio address that he made on a national hook-up he made the following argument in its behalf:

Favoring the complete separation of powers, executive, judicial and legislative, I naturally believe it is time to stop these judicial usurpations brought about according to statements of their own judicial colleagues by the economic falacies of a majority of the Supreme Court. To do this I favor using all the powers necessary to accomplish the purpose which were given to the Congress by the wise framers of the Constitution. Our Constitution can only be preserved by leaving each department of government free to exercise the powers given it and no more. A majority of our judges should not amend our Constitution according to their economic predilections every time they decide a case. By such action they block the orderly and necessary progress of the people and jeopardize our most sacred rights and liberties. Our democracy can work out its own problems within our Constitution if the rights of human beings as human beings are given first importance and if our Constitution is not so misinterpreted and altered as to shackle the democratic processes themselves. . . . Great modern problems still confront us. Our Constitution contemplates that the people shall solve them. They can and will do so if our Courts abandon their unconstitutional interpretation of our Constitution.[9]

It seems pretty clear that Black's emotions played an important part in his adoption of political principles. He was for the underdog from the time a fight started, and there is no reason to doubt the sincerity of his belief that one of the functions of government is to equalize as far as possible the opportunities of all citizens. Big men, he seemed to think, were inclined to impose upon little men, and big institutions were a menace because of their very bigness. Like the inventor of Colt's revolver, he longed to equip the people with weapons that would make all men the same height.

This was the light reflected from the purely legislative side of Senator Black's congressional career. The larger part of his public reputation, however, arose from activities that but indirectly relate to actual law-making and which are justified in legislative procedure only upon the theory that light thrown in dark places may reveal what needs to be eradicated from the law or added to reinforce its purposes. It was in this field of investigation that Senator Black first attracted national notice.

CHAPTER IV

LANTERN AND SCOURGE

The new Senator from Alabama had not been long in Washington before he began to notice certain irregularities that aroused his suspicion. Whether his experience as prosecuting attorney had developed in him a sharp sense of the suspicious or whether there was a scepticism inherent in his make-up, it did not take him long to ferret out matters that seemed to him to demand legislative examination. When he approached the United States Shipping Board to obtain consideration for a Mobile shipping company he is said to have sensed corruption, inefficiency, and waste in that agency's operation, and in 1928 he made the headlines by holding up an appropriation bill in a futile attempt to limit the salaries of Shipping Board officials. In 1929 he introduced a resolution authorizing an investigation of the lobbyists and their activities but the Republican-dominated Senate was in no mood to permit an upstart malcontent from the opposition ranks to initiate an inquiry that might be so far-reaching.

It was not until the Democratic administration came to power that the opportunity he had been seeking materialized. Both the Senate and the President were now ready to give their blessing to any investigation that might serve the dual purpose of promoting the public interest and further embarrassing the already discredited Republican administration. So when Black in 1933 renewed his fight upon the Shipping Board and introduced a

52

resolution authorizing an investigation of its activities and the government's methods of awarding mail-carrying contracts, the resolution was speedily passed; and according to Senate custom the author of the resolution was named chairman of the investigating committee.

The ocean mail contracts were the first to be scrutinized, and although a number of embarrassing irregularities were brought to light in this connection the shocking facts remained to be uncovered in an inquiry into the air mail contracts and subsidies. One of the first of a series of startling disclosures came when a post-office clerk testified that during the last days of the Hoover administration, under the orders of Postmaster General Walter F. Brown, he had burned many of the official records concerning these contracts.[1] Thereupon Brown himself hurried to Washington with two packets which he delivered personally to his successor, Postmaster-General Farley. These, he explained, he had found quite unexpectedly among his personal files where they had no doubt been inadvertently placed while he was preparing to leave office. Along with this remark, however, he dropped the barbed words that they might have been "surreptiously placed among my personal papers at the instigation of someone who was engaged in a conspiracy of character assassination," [2] and added that he had some evidence to support this theory. He denied that he had ever ordered any clerk to dispose of government files.

In spite of this disclaimer and denial, the public suspected that everything in connection with Brown's administration of the Postmaster General's office had not been wholly above board, and both Roosevelt and Black recognized the opportunity offered by a

53

thorough investigation. The President publicly advised the Senator to go the limit, and this the Senator was delighted to do. Piece by piece he fitted together a story of political graft, favoritism, and bribery in the allotment of air-mail contracts.

It was disclosed that 90 per cent of the subsidy was received by four large companies, the so-called "aviation trust." Officers of independent airlines testified that they had not even been able to put in bids during Brown's incumbency, and others related how they did underbid such big favorites as the American Airways but never could get a contract. It came out that in two years Postmaster-General Brown had given American Airways 4,414 miles of route extensions without any pretense at competitive bidding and had awarded the North American group 2,516 miles in the same generous manner.[3]

In Brown's defense it was pointed out that there was no law which required competitive bidding and that during his administration air transport had greatly improved. His friends insisted that he should be judged by the over-all picture of air mail progress rather than by separated mistakes dug up here and there by the investigating committee. Public approval was with the committee. "A favorite has no friends," especially after his party has suffered a political reverse, and there was little doubt that the big airlines had long basked in the warmth of the Hoover administration's partiality. Not since the days of Teapot Dome had a cabinet officer been so badly compromised as was the former Postmaster General.

Finally in January 1934 the President exercised his authority to cancel all existing air-mail contracts and announced that henceforth the United States Army would carry the mail until such a time as a fair and satisfactory plan for letting contracts to private companies could be worked out. In justification of the executive's act Postmaster General Farley charged that his predecessor had awarded contracts illegally and had encouraged collusion among the big airlines which regularly had agreed among themselves not to compete with each other by bidding for mail contracts upon the same lines. Senator Black in a nation-wide broadcast described the situation thus:

Since 1925 taxpayers of this nation have paid $1,143,255,705 for the development of aviation. The tragic part of this picture is that investigations have revealed recently that these huge governmental expenditures have, in great part, found their way into the pockets of profiteers, stock manipulators, political and powerful financial groups who never flew a plane, who never invented an engine, who never improved an airplane part. In short this great and indispensable industry was greedily grabbed away from the control of those interested in aviation progress, and has been utilized by profiteers as a means for private gain through stock jobbing, speculation and monopoly.[4]

It was at this point that wind and weather began to interfere with the Black campaign of public persuasion. If the Army had succeeded in carry the mails as army officials had assured the President it could do, the public in all probability would have approved the President's action and would have considered that the "aviation trust" had suffered no more than just retribution. But the army was not competent to fulfill its promise. Army fliers, totally untrained for the work they were now called to do, began to crash in rapid succession. In the course of a few weeks public indignation had risen against Roosevelt's administration which was now accused of sacrificing young lives for the sake of political advantage.

Arthur Krock noted in the New York *Times* that for the first time since his inauguration the President's administration was actually on the defensive.[5] *Time* magazine in a bitter report of the continuing casualties would describe the death of an army pilot and then add a paragraph like this:

Inside the Senate Office Building at Washington all was snug and warm as Senator Black badgered onetime Postmaster General Brown about air mail contracts which the Administration had cancelled for fraud and collusion.

After this would come the description of another fatal crash along with which a note of this sort would be added:

At a dinner in balmy Savannah General Farley explained that the Administration's air policy would end abuses which grew out of an unfair and stifling competition.[6]

Whether the facts or the criticism became too much for the President he was soon desirous of checking the course of accumulating proof of the army's incapacity to do the job it had undertaken. In less than a month from the time that the duty of carrying the mails was turned over to the army the President directed that it be at once turned back to private enterprise.

Despite the criticism it occasioned and the trouble it caused the Roosevelt administration the Black investigation finally resulted in substantial improvement in the methods of handling air-mail contracts. The Postmaster General was now required to award contracts to the lowest responsible bidders, and unsuccessful bidders were given the right to appeal to the Comptroller General. Each carrier was restricted to three contracts.[7]

The long-favored airlines protested bitterly against these changes. All the larger aviation companies declared them to be highly impractical but nevertheless they were put into effect and the result of competitive bidding was apparent at once. Some companies now bid to carry mail as low as 17½ cents per airplane mile in contrast with the rates that the Post Office Department had formerly fixed at from 41 to 45 cents for the same service.

Throughout the conduct of the investigation Senator Black had shown the technique of a shrewd, experienced prosecuting attorney. Incidentally, he had stepped upon many Republican toes in the process of examination, and anti-administration papers continued to insist that the true object of his questioning was not to disclose fraud against the public but to discredit men he did not like. *Time* hinted that he had persuaded the President against his better judgment to cancel the air-mail contracts and that such insistence had sprung from a desire to keep alive public interest in the investigation.[8] The manner in which Black conducted this investigation might have seemed high-handed to some of the embarrassed witnesses but general opinion appeared to approve it. Convinced that a good deal of shady work had gone on, the public was not squeamish about methods used to expose it.

When William P. McCracken, an attorney for one of the favored airlines, was subpoenaed by the Black committee he refused to show his private files on the ground of the confidential relationship of attorney and client.[9] Senator Black suggested that McCracken wire his clients for permission to open his files and this he readily agreed to do. While the committee was waiting for him to report the reply of his clients, however, he allowed agents of the companies he represented to go through his files and remove any correspondence they did not want the committee to have. Then when Mr. McCracken was again summoned by the committee he refused to appear and denied the committee's right to employ compulsory process to require his presence.

Senator Black immediately offered a resolution directing the Senate Sergeant at Arms to arrest McCracken and bring him before the bar of the chamber. The obdurate McCracken was taken into custody along with an airline official who had removed some of the papers from McCracken's files. Both were sentenced to ten days in jail. The airline official submitted at once, but McCracken sought relief through the courts.[10] In the end he likewise served his sentence.

It was not until he was under way with his investigation of lobbying activities that Senator Black and his methods ran afoul of general public opinion. Always suspicious of lobbyists and a foe of the powerful public utilities, the Senator found the situation in which these utilities were accused of undue lobbying just to his taste. Second now only to Senator Norris in his advocacy of public experiment in the field of utility ownership, he had taken a leading part in the bitter debate on the Utility Holding Company bill embracing the so-called "Death Sentence" clause requiring utility holding companies to divest themselves of their interests in all but a single integrated group of operating companies.

In the summer of 1935 Senator Black introduced a resolution calling for a Senate investigation of the lobbying activities of the utility companies. While still in committee the scope of the proposed investigation was broadened so that its duty would be to investigate any lobbying affecting any kind of legislation.

The investigation opened with a spectacular move when one morning in July an officer appeared at the office door of Philip Gadsden, the chairman of an organization known as the Public Utilities Executives, and marched him off to the hearing without prior notice or opportunity to make preparation. According to one reporter five minutes after Gadsden's arrival Chairman Black threw open the doors of the committee room and cried jovially, "Tell the boys of the press to come in. The show is about to begin." [11] And so it was.

While the examination of this witness was taking place Senator Black's aides were busily engaged in making another kind of examination. In the office from which the chairman of the Public Utilities Executives had been removed by subpoena agents of Senator Black's committee searched his files, both official and personal. This procedure provoked Mr. Gadsden, a mild-mannered South Carolinian, to make a furious attack upon Black. "They actually went through my personal checkbook," he told reporters, "I think it's an outrage." [12] A good many observers felt the same way. In the New York *Times* Arthur Krock predicted that "private lives and personal liberties will be raided again as if the Czarist police were operating." [13] It was suggested that the purpose of Senator Black's sudden opening of his "show" was to jump the gun on a House committee which was also investigating lobbying activities and hold first place in the headlines. Chairman O'Connor of the House committee was reported to resent bitterly Black's impetuous intervention.

Despite criticism of the Senate committee's methods, it was soon apparent that it had unearthed a rich store of carefully concealed fact and circumstance and that more had been wrought by lobbying than the people dreamed. Mr. Gadsden admitted that the utilities had spent $301,865 to fight the Holding Company bill.[14] A few days later an advertising man employed by the utilities admitted that he had suggested political methods to certain utility officials, one of which was that a whispering campaign be launched to create the popular impression that President Roosevelt was insane.[15] It was disclosed that Howard Hopson, who controlled the Associated Gas and Electric Company, had drawn $2,805,000 from the company from 1929 to 1933 and that during much of this time the company had paid its stockholders no dividends.[16]

Representative Driscoll reported that he had received 816 telegrams opposing the utilities bill, all from Warren, Pennsylvania. The fact that 114 of the names began with the letter B and that one friend of the Congressman when asked about the telegram bearing his name denied any knowledge of it,[17] started the committee upon an investigation of telegraph company records. One employee of the Western Union Telegraph Company testified that great numbers of fake messages had been filed, signed often with names read out of city directories;[18] another admitted that in violation of the Federal Communication Commission's regulation that duplicates of telegrams were to be kept for one year, he had burned certain files after the investigation began.[19] According to Senator Black it was shown that the utilities had engaged in enough dirty work to keep twenty committees busy.[20]

However, with no more than two committees digging in the

same field conflict could not be avoided. Both the Senate Committee and the House Committee were searching at the same time for Mr. Hopson of Associated Gas and Electric. Chairman O'Connor's committee found him first and it was rumored that the quarry and his friends had so arranged it in order that he might fall into the hands of O'Connor rather than Black.

As Mr. Hopson left the session of the House Committee he found a Senate Committee officer waiting, subpoena in hand, to take him before the Senate Committee. Service of the process was prevented, however, presumably by agents of Chairman O'Connor, who heatedly declared that his committee would not release Hopson to the Senators until it was done with him and that the action of the Senate Committee was a "direct affront to the House of Representatives." [20]

On the afternoon he finished testifying before the House Committee Mr. Hopson walked over to the Senate Committee's room and announced that he was ready to submit himself to questioning. If he had expected rougher treatment at Black's hands than at those of O'Connor, he was not disappointed. Senator Black cut the witness off sharply when he attempted explanations with his answers and within a few minutes outdid the O'Connor examination with results obtained. Finally Mr. Hopson, who theretofore had made quite a reputation for shrewdness and ability to take care of himself under fire, threw in the sponge and said to his inquisitor, "You have me on the hip." [21]

During the congressional recess Senator Black and his aides worked in further preparation for the hearings notwithstanding the fact that the Utility Holding Company bill that had prompted

61

the investigation in the first place had already been passed. When the Black committee resumed its probe in the spring of 1936 its first action to make the headlines was its demand upon the Western Union Telegraph Company for its files containing the thousands of telegrams sent during the earlier period of the investigation. A number of prominent lawyers at once disputed the committee's right to employ compulsory process to cast such a general dragnet among the papers of the corporation. It was insisted that such a "blanket" seizure of papers was a violation of the Fourth Amendment to the Constitution in that a search that did not specify the nature of the thing sought for was unreasonable. A subpoena to bring documents, it was pointed out, could not be used in aid of a mere "fishing expedition" in order that the committee might look for further clues and signs of misdoing. It was also charged that the committee's demand ignored the time-honored veil of professional privilege behind which a lawyer's correspondence with his client was properly shielded from the eyes of the curious.

These issues were brought before the courts by the move of Silas Hardy Strawn, a former president of the American Bar Association and a bitter critic of the New Deal. When this Chicago lawyer found that the committee had issued a subpoena for all the telegrams sent and received by his office during a fixed period he immediately sought an injunction restraining the telegraph company from furnishing such papers to the committee. The fact that the number of telegrams sought by the committee was estimated at five million seems to justify the charge that the committee's search was a general one.

To such criticism Senator Black replied: "We've subpoenaed all the telegrams of these gentlemen who conceal themselves behind organizations and groups in order to determine the policies of the nation behind a mask." [22]   In a speech on the floor of the Senate he warned the courts against issuing any such injunction as Mr. Strawn had asked.   He said:.

I will state very frankly that, in my judgment, if any judge ever issued an injunction to prevent delivery of papers that were sought by this body through subpoena, the Congress should immediately enact legislation taking away that jurisdiction from the courts. Congress creates the jurisdiction of those courts. . . . If I had ever had any idea that any judge would issue an injunction against this body's getting certain evidence, I would long ago have introduced a bill to take away the jurisdiction which enabled the court to do that.[23]

The daily press now bristled with such expressions as "Nazi," "pillage," "terrorism," "espionage," "gestapo tactics," and the like. Senator Black's support by the Ku Klux Klan was recalled to show that he was running true to Klan form, and the New York *Times* remarked that it was not surprised to hear from Washington that the Senate Chamber had "a smell, lingering and humorous, of boiling oil and melted lead." [24]

When Strawn's injunction suit came to be heard in court the Senate Committee through its attorney contended that the legislative body was the exclusive judge of the propriety and validity of its subpoenas just as the courts were the judge of theirs. With somewhat more unction than Senator Black had used he intimated that a very unfortunate conflict might arise should the court undertake to restrain Western Union from delivering the telegrams called for by the committee. However, neither this argument nor

63

Black's threat impressed Justice Wheat of the District of Columbia Supreme Court before whom the matter was argued. "Feeling as I do," he said, "that this subpoena goes way beyond any legitimate exercise of the right of *subpoena duces tecum,* I think I am bound to grant the injunction." [25] So Mr. Strawn's telegrams remained undisturbed in the Western Union files.

Encouraged by this decision William Randolph Hearst now plunged into the fray and the headlines and sought an injunction to restrain the telegraph company from turning over to the committee a telegram that he had sent to one of his editorial writers suggesting an idea for some anti-Roosevelt editorials. It was obvious that Mr. Hearst, however, was actuated by a newspaper man's instincts rather than a lawyer's, for while his suit was enough like the Strawn suit to ride into the news upon the current of interest the former case had created, it was very unlike it in the single determinative question of fact upon which that case had been decided. In Strawn's case the committee had sought to have delivered to it all communications of the plaintiff so that it could look through them to see what it could find. In Hearst's case a certain and specifically described telegram had been called for and there was no reason to object to the demand upon the ground of its generality. When the court dismissed his suit Hearst turned from the forum of the court to that of the people and launched in his papers a vitriolic attack upon what he termed the "Blackguard Committee."

In defense of the actions of his committee Senator Black wrote an article that was published in *Harper's Magazine* entitled "Inside a Senate Investigation." In answer to the protests that his committee had invaded private rights he said:

64

Unwillingness to answer questions, often under the unwise advice of lawyers, makes it necessary for committee investigators to examine personal files and papers. . . . Frequently the persons asked to reveal their papers protest earnestly that the documents in question are purely personal. It is amazing how much "purely personal correspondence" there is in business files. This is an old dodge and was settled ages ago.[26]

Legislative investigating committees armed with the power of subpoena and search, he said, were the only instruments capable of exposing the machinations of unscrupulous groups that throve in darkness and could only be destroyed by the rays of "pitiless publicity."

In spite of the pitiless publicity that Senator Black had turned upon certain of these unscrupulous groups his investigation did not have the effect of accomplishing the legislation he sponsored. An anti-lobby bill that would have required lobbyists to register their aims and names with Congress and to make a monthly report of how much they were spending was overwhelmingly rejected by the House of Representatives apparently still smarting from the insult it had sustained in the Hopson incident. Futhermore certain members and their friends had been even more incensed by the fact that Senator Black had dragged forth from one lobbyist the admission that he had lived in a house in Washington with six representatives and been a sort of Goodtime Charlie to many others.[27]

The foregoing resumé of Hugo Black's public career before his appointment to the Supreme Court seems fairly to permit certain generalizations. Obviously he was characterized by a vitality that manifested itself in extraordinary activity both physical and mental. His opponents in the Alabama primaries could testify to his tireless campaigning, and this ability for sustained effort was quite as marked after he had taken his seat in the Senate. It was this vigor that made possible his continued self-education and his retention of general interests in spite of the heavy demands of official duties.

In his legislative career there is no basis for the conclusion that his processes of thought were unusually profound, although there is abundant reason to observe that they were quick and alert. His language does not reflect a precision of thought and logic that often marks the man whose mind works with machine-like accuracy. What it does show are the gaps and overlaps that word arrangement always suffers when the speed of thought taxes the flexibility of the tongue. It cannot be justly said that in his speech he was careless, but it was plain that when words had been made to serve their purpose in conveying thought he was not greatly concerned with the excellence of their selection nor the artistry of their arrangement.

As words were but the means to an end so were the rules of law. No scruples of a judicial conscience forbade him to skirt the limits of the permissible and go quite as far as the tether of technical rules could be stretched. Power, he seemed to think, was something to be made the most of, and it never occurred to him that there need be an apology for so using it.

Politicians who continually champion the cause of the common man and harp upon the wrongs of the proletariat are always accused of being demagogues, and oftentimes they are. Black was so accused but a review of his record does not warrant the charge. He did not act the part of the typical demagogue who is as careful not to get ahead of popular thought as he is to keep up with it. Neither was he inclined to make friends with mammon when his opposition to it had apparently accomplished his purpose. Certainly the safest course politically would have been to accept the support of the Alabama Power Company after he had been elected to the Senate. Instead of adding it to the train of his political followers, however, he deliberately adopted a course that made the potent private utility corporation his implacable enemy.

It is not to be gainsaid that he was a political strategist. He had mastered the game of politics and worked hard to win at it. He was able somehow to win the support of the state Ku Klux organization notwithstanding the national leadership's promise of its support to an opponent, and he was careful to refrain from an expression on a prohibition referendum while there was danger that the prohibition vote could be alienated to an adversary. But political strategy lacks something of being outright hypocrisy and nothing in Black's career deserves this characterization.

Possibly his silence for so long after the Ku Klux issue was raised is the nearest thing his record shows to studied deceit. It is true that he kept silent when an expression would have been damaging, and it is not to be doubted that he kept silent because of this fact. Again, however, he must be judged in the light of all the circumstances and as a man rather than a demi-god. At any rate there is no evidence that he ever denied his Klan affiliation although certainly he did not expose it.

In summation it could be said by a reasonably objective observer that Justice Black's appointment placed upon the Supreme Court an alert and ambitious member of pronounced social, political and economic views, positive, uncompromising and self-assured.

CHAPTER V

NEW WINE

Considering the furor his appointment had occasioned and the trouble it had caused the Roosevelt administration it might reasonably have been expected that once on the bench Justice Black would have tried, for at least an interval, to make himself inconspicuous. He might have voted consistently with the liberal wing of the Court, thereby fulfilling the purpose for which he had been appointed, but without calling any particular attention to himself. This was not the course adopted by Hugo Black. On the contrary, he often struck out alone, and sometimes in directions that not even the most liberal of the older justices had theretofore suggested.

By contending that the word "person" as used in the Fourteenth Amendment did not include corporations,[1] by ridiculing the formula for utility rate-making that had been in effect since 1898,[2] and by attacking the doctrine that there could be a federal court interpretation of the common law separate and apart from that adopted by the state courts,[3] he focused upon himself not only the attention of those who regularly follow the activities of the Supreme Court, but many who ordinarily accord them scant notice.

Sixteen times during his first term he spoke as a dissenter, and on twelve of these occasions he spoke alone. In ten cases where he concurred in the result he either disagreed with some of the Court's reasoning or preferred to reach the same conclusion on other grounds. Only the two irreconcilables, McReynolds and Butler, dissented more frequently.[4]

His first opinion indicated that judicial office had worked little change in his manner of forthright and vehement speech and that his judicial robe did not blot out his characteristic flashes of emotion. This case involved no matter of great importance nor called for any deep learning in the law, yet both the conclusion reached and the method of reaching it were so typical of its author's habits of thought that it may be considered an appropriate introduction to his judicial philosophy.

The Court upheld an order of the Federal Trade Commission that three sharpers cease and desist from their practice of hoodwinking gullible members of the public by a time-worn pretense and a little bald-faced lying.[5] The Federal Trade Commission had discovered that book agents of an encyclopedia publishing company were playing upon the vanity of their prospects with the tale that their company was seeking out selected individuals for the purpose of giving them a set of encyclopedias and that the only return asked of the persons so favored was the privilege of using their names for advertising purposes and reference.

Quite naturally the publishers who were spending their advertising appropriations in sending agents out to give away sets of books wished to select as donees only such persons as were sufficiently interested in the books to desire to keep them up-to-date by subscribing for a loose-leaf extension service that would keep them current for ten years. The agents explained that the price of this extension service was only $69.50 so that the favored persons selected to receive the gift were getting for this small payment a set of books and a service that regularly sold for between $150 and $200, a statement that the Federal Trade Commission found quite divergent from the truth.

The Court of Appeals had sustained the Federal Trade Commission in ordering the book company not to represent falsely to prospective purchasers that sets of books had been reserved to be given away to selected persons, but reversed the Commission's order that it cease to represent that it was giving away the books and charging only for the loose-leaf extension service. In arriving at its conclusion the Court of Appeals said:

We cannot take seriously the suggestion that a man who is buying a set of books and a ten year's 'extension service' will be fatuous enough to be misled by the mere statement that the first are given away, and that he is paying only for the second. . . . Such trivial niceties are too impalpable for practical affairs, they are will-o'-the-wisps which divert attention from substantial evils.[6]

Many courts have reasoned likewise and lawbooks are full of explanations and examples of the rule that purchasers of merchandise must look out for themselves when glib-tongued vendors ply their trade. Long ago there was grafted upon the law of deceit the doctrine of *caveat emptor* that requires a prospective purchaser to see and know the reasonably obvious or hold his peace thereafter. Frequently the logic of the rule had been criticized on the ground that it denies the law's relief to the man who needs it most by requiring of him a standard of judgment beyond that with which he is endowed.

Justice Black, who throughout both his professional and political careers had generally represented that class of society most often the victim of deception and oppression, had no patience with the view that a purchaser's credulity and naïveté might be used as an excuse by one who had imposed upon him. Laws, he said, were made to protect the trusting as well as the suspicious, and the fact that a claim might seem obviously false to some did not change its character nor take away its power to deceive others less sophisticated. Then verging toward a vehemence that might have characterized a district attorney castigating a defendant charged with obtaining money under false pretenses, he concluded that "the rule of *caveat emptor* should not be relied upon to reward fraud and deception," [7] and hence upheld the ruling of the Federal Trade Commission.

The first Black opinion to attact general notice was a lone dissent from a *per curiam* holding of the Court.[8] The small flash of wrath that had been called down by book agents duping a few credulous victims was nothing to the burst of denunciation and ridicule with which he attacked the doctrine that allowed federal courts to review rates set by state utility commissions. There could have been for him no subject more provocative.

In 1931 the City of Indianapolis had petitioned the Indiana Public Service Commission to reduce the rates charged small consumers by the Indianapolis Water Company. The Commission fixed the rate in December 1932 and the water company, charging that the rate was confiscatory, appealed to the courts for relief. In November 1935 the District Court held that there had been no confiscation; in March 1937 the Circuit Court of Appeals held that there had been confiscation; and in January 1938 the Supreme Court sent the case back to the District Court for trial anew. Such

71

a situation, Black thought, was intolerable and convincing proof that judicial review of the rulings of state utility commissions was making a travesty of their efforts at rate regulation.

In the year 1898 in the case of Smyth *v.* Ames[9] the Supreme Court had opened the door to judicial review of state regulation of public utility rates by saying:

While rates for transportation of persons and property within the limits of the state are primarily for its determination, the question of whether they are so unreasonably low as to deprive the carrier of its property without such compensation as the Constitution secures, and therefore, without due process of law, cannot be so conclusively determined by the legislature of the state, or by regulations adopted under its authority, that the matter may not become the subject of judicial inquiry.[10]

The basis of calculation as to the reasonableness of rates was to be "the fair value of the property being used by it for the convenience of the public." [11]

No sooner were the words spoken than the Court seemed to realize that the term "fair value" might be an elusive sort of measure, for who could place an estimate of "fair value" upon public service corporations that exercised natural or state protected monopoly and seldom became the subject of barter and sale? So the Court conveniently provided this formula:

In order to ascertain that value, the original cost of construction, the amount expended in permanent improvements, the amount and the market value of its bonds and stock, the present as compared with the original cost of construction, the probable earning capacity of the property under particular rates prescribed by statute, and the sum required to meet operating expenses, are all matters for consideration, and are to be given such weight as may be just and right in each case.[12]

Since the Court failed to furnish any additional formula for finding what weight to be given the several factors would be "just and right in each case," every utility lawyer set out to prove in his particular rate case that it was "just and right" to accord the greatest weight to that particular factor most likely to advantage his client.

Out of the welter of rate cases came diverse names for concepts of what should constitute "fair value." One theory stressed the "historical cost," another the "replacement cost," still another the "reproduction cost," and finally, under the name of the "prudent investment theory" the measure of "fair value" was said to be the amount of capital contributed by investors and prudently used in the construction and operation of utility property.

Of all these the "reproduction cost" theory was conceived with the greatest degree of artificiality and allowed the most latitude for guess and speculation. That theory required an hypothesis that a plant which had been built up over many years and under widely varying conditions had somehow become nonexistent, and that someone for some unfathomable reason desired to reconstruct it exactly as it was, disdaining to make use of scientific improvements or concede anything to the toll of time.

For example when the spreading chestnut tree still shaded the village smithy and bloomed and bore on countless hillsides, chestnut timber was considered ideal for telephone poles, a great number of which were still of that wood long after the chestnut blight had made living chestnut trees no more than a memory. Since a new chestnut pole could be obtained hardly anywhere and only at an exorbitant price, it can be seen what an estimate of "reproduction cost," strictly applied, would have led to in valuing the

73

property of a telephone company that forty years before had built its lines with chestnut timber. Such an absurd insistence was perhaps never actually made before a rate-fixing body, but it varied only in degree from the contention made in many cases where it was argued that the "reproduction cost" test must not be departed from. The ramifications of this concept reduced most rate cases to a maze of figures in which commissions and courts were hopelessly lost, but within which hundreds of professional appraisers, accountants, engineers, expert witnesses and lawyers throve and fattened.

The expense of making evaluations reached enormous proportions, and since it was a legitimate expense which the utility had the right to pass along to the public no utility was at much pains to restrict it. When the City of New York initiated its rate case against the New York Edison Company, that corporation's expenditure for appraising, accounting and legal fees was over $4,000,000.[13] It was reported that the New York Telephone Company topped this figure by another million in preparing its appraisal for presentation before a regulatory body.[14] But perhaps the appraisal to end appraisals was that which Congress ordered the Interstate Commerce Commission to make of American railroad property and which at the time of a hearing before the House Committee on Interstate and Foreign Commerce in 1932 had been going on for eighteen years and had cost the Commission and the railroads $178,000,000.[15]

With such sums of money available it was no wonder that a rate case was the kind of game seldom finished at candlelight. No body had any reason to kill a goose that was laying such an abund-

74

ance of golden eggs for appraisers, accountants, engineers, expert witnesses and lawyers—that is, nobody except the public.

Thus "Roland to the dark tower came" and in a lone dissent sounded the death knell of an era in judicial history. The rule laid down in Smyth *v.* Ames was doomed.[16] The facts marshalled in Black's opinion were shocking to the public conscience. His argument was irrefutable, his sarcasm scathing, and his logic clear and convincing. Commenting upon the "complete unreliability" of the reproduction cost theory, he said:

Wherever the question of utility valuation arises today, it is exceedingly difficult to discern the truth through the maze of formulas and the jungle of metaphysical concepts sometimes conceived, and often fostered, by the ingenuity of those who seek inflated valuations to support excessive rates. Even the testimony of engineers, with wide experience in developing this theory and expounding it to courts, is not in agreement as to the meaning of the vague and uncertain terms created to add invisible and intangible values to actual physical property. Completely lost in the confusion of language—too frequently invented for the purpose of confusing—commissions and courts passing upon rates for public utilities are driven to listen to conjectures, speculations, estimates and guesses, all under the name of "reproduction costs." [17]

Then moving rapidly on from his attack upon the theory of valuation, Black announced a position that was an even more radical departure from established precedent. "I believe," he said, "the State of Indiana has the right to regulate the price of water in Indianapolis free from interference by federal courts." [18]

This dissent was proof positive to the minds of the utility lawyers that there was much more the matter with the new Justice than membership in the Ku Klux Klan or even too eager an inclination to employ *subpoenas duces tecum.* On the other hand, much favorable comment resulted. According to Walton Hamilton, professor of Constitutional Law at Yale University, the dissent was a " hopeful symbol " and a " wholesome prophesy," that would "liberate administrative bodies from slavery to archaic ceremonials and leave them free to shape ways and means to the end they are expected to serve." [19] If there were a prize for the best opinion of the year, he declared, it should go to Black for his dissent in this case.

The opinion, however, that in the minds of conservatives was to stamp Justice Black as a thorough revolutionary and end all hope that he might be tamed by judicial environment was his one-man dissent in the case of Connecticut General Life Insurance Company *v.* Johnson,[20] wherein, upon the maxim that nothing is ever settled until it is settled right, he dared reopen the long decided question of whether a corporation was a person in such a sense as to bring it under the protection of the Fourteenth Amendment. This question he answered with a ringing negative. As an historical matter there was nothing new in the view he took, for he was but reiterating a story pretty well established in the minds of historians. But to incorporate the same in a judicial opinion was to commit the offense of "unsettling the law" in the minds of those who think it more important that law should be established than that it should be right or reasonable.

The case involved the validity of a California statute which operated to tax a foreign insurance company on premiums received in another state on reinsurance contracts effected and payable in the other state. Apart from Justice Cardozo who took no part in the consideration of the case, all members of the Court except Black agreed that the effecting of the reinsurance contracts outside the State of California constituted no privilege, business or property on which the State of California could levy a tax and that the effort to do so constituted an attempt to take the corporation's property without due process of law. Justice Black's dissent revived arguments that the Supreme Court had undertaken to lay at rest a half century earlier. He asserted that a corporation was not a person within the meaning of the Fourteenth Amendment.

Lawyers could sit at home in the evenings and read with academic interest and without excitement how John A. Bingham and Roscoe Conkling had schemed to insinuate into a constitutional amendment a single word [21] that was to become the key to what one eminent historian called "a fundamental revolution in the Constitution." [22] Over coffee cups they could discuss without rancor the so-called "conspiracy theory" of the origin of the Amendment, but they felt that in doing so they were dealing with the dry bones of history, and that their differences upon the subject had no more practical application to the settlement of modern problems than did the question of whether Jefferson Davis was correct in his position upon the right of secession. As the War Between the States had answered the one question, so, they considered, the Supreme Court had determined the other. In 1886 Chief Justice Waite during the argument of the case of Santa Clara County v. Southern Pacific Railroad Company[23] had said, "The Court does not wish to hear argument on the question whether the provision of the Fourteenth Amendment . . . applies to these corporations. We are of the opinion that it does." [24]

It would have been a bold advocate thereafter who would have raised the question in presenting a case. A member of the tribunal, however, speaks from a better vantage point, and Justice Black did not hesitate to say as a judge what it would have been poor policy to suggest as an advocate. Though the matter set forth in his dissent was not novel, it was logically arranged and convincingly stated. His conclusion was simply that, " neither the history nor the language of the Fourteenth Amendment justifies the belief that corporations are included within its protection." [25] He argued, however, not as an activist, seeking to have the Court enter new fields of philosophy, but as a prophet calling the people back to the faith of their fathers:

If the people of this nation wish to deprive the States of their sovereign rights to determine what is a fair and just tax upon corporations doing a purely local business within their own state boundaries, there is a way provided by the Constitution to accomplish this purpose. That way does not lie along the course of judicial amendment to that fundamental charter. An amendment having that purpose could be submitted by Congress as provided by the Constitution. I do not believe that the Fourteenth Amendment had that purpose, nor that the people believed it had that purpose, nor that it should be construed as having that purpose.[26]

Comments were about what reasonably might have been expected—stirred mostly by feeling upon the economic effect of reopening an old question rather than by any objective view of the dissenter's logic. Conservatives did not say, " Here is a Daniel come to judgment who opposes judicial legislation and wants to destroy the effect of that which has already altered our written Constitution." And liberals did not say, "Alas, we have elevated to the Bench a strict constructionist whose views make the Constitution static and inflexible." On the contrary, each group read the dissent through glasses colored by what they wished on the one hand, or feared on the other.

Some observers who could not deny the factual basis of Black's thesis and who agreed with him concerning the misuse of the due process clause, nevertheless criticized him for making too abrupt an about face. He had, they declared, violated " a fundamental canon of judicial craftsmanship," by failing to approach his position " gradually and by intimation." [27]

If, however, such critics could have looked forward a few weeks they would have visioned the Court executing an about-face movement upon a rule of law that was old when the Fourteenth Amendment was born. Moreover, the only intimating upon the matter had been done a few weeks earlier by Justice Black in a lone dissent. The rule that was overturned was the one laid down in Swift v. Tyson[28] in 1842 and which, if Justice Butler accurately stated the matter, had been in force "since the foundation of the Government." [29] This was the doctrine that federal courts exercising jurisdiction on the ground of diversity of citizenship need not in matters of general jurisprudence apply the unwritten law of the state as declared by its highest court, but are free to exercise an independent judgment as to what the common law of the state is—or ought to be. Even justices who in dissents had looked askance at the doctrine had come to accept it as completely settled, and Justice Holmes who criticized it had once said, "I should leave Swift v. Tyson undisturbed . . . but I would not allow it to spread the assumed dominion into new fields." [30]

Justice Black, however, showed no such disposition to tolerate a rule he disapproved. At the first opportunity he voted to cast it aside.[31] The case which arose in Montana presented the question of whether a man had died by suicide or accident, a question made pertinent by the fact that his insurance policy provided for double indemnity in the event of accidental death. In every state and in the federal courts there is a presumption against suicide. The question upon which there is little general agreement is how much evidence is necessary to remove such a presumption, some courts holding that upon the slightest evidence the presumption disappears, and some requiring a more substantial amount. The State of Montana adopted the rule that unless the evidence all pointed to suicide "with such certainty as to preclude any other reasonable hypothesis," [32] the presumption against self-destruction continued.

The federal court to which the case had been removed by reason of diversity of citizenship did not adopt the Montana interpretation, although in this particular case it found for the plaintiff. When the case reached the Supreme Court Justice Butler delivered the majority opinion reversing the judgment of the district court on the ground of erroneous instructions and apparently assumed that what the Montana state courts had to say on such subjects as the amount of evidence required to establish a fact amounted to nothing when a case was tried in the federal jurisdiction.

This, in Justice Black's judgment, was vicious error and he vigorously struck at it. It was his opinion that Montana had the right to follow whatever theory she chose and that federal courts sitting in that jurisdiction should give effect to the law as they found it there. Although this dissent was joined by no other justice, it foreshadowed the early destruction of a great mass of federal common law interpretation that had sprung from the seeds sown by Justice Story nearly one hundred years before.

To those who were beginning to suspect that Justice Black's opinions in cases involving corporations sprang less from his concern with protecting the power of the states than with restricting the power of corporations, the case of Indiana *ex rel.* Anderson *v.* Brand[33] gave pause. This case arose when the State of Indiana repealed a statute providing permanent tenure for township teachers. A teacher who was employed while the statute was in effect was dismissed after its repeal. Thereupon she brought suit charging the impairment of contract, a contention which the Supreme Court upheld. Justice Black alone dissented.

"In my opinion," he said, "this reversal unconstitutionally limits the right of Indiana to control Indiana's public school system." [34] Pointing out that the Supreme Court of Indiana, construing the state law, had held that it did not give teachers definite and permanent contracts but was only intended as a limitation upon the plenary power of local school officials to cancel contracts, and that the Indiana Supreme Court's construction of the meaning of an Indiana statute must be accepted, he took sharp issue with the Court in favor of the state's right to undo what it had done.

Some four months later in another unsupported dissenting opinion he defended a statute from the same state which had been said by a majority of the Court to be an unconstitutional burden upon interstate commerce.[35] In both the form and sub-

81

stance of this dissent Black attained an excellence of judicial expression he had not reached theretofore.

The Indiana legislature had enacted a tax upon the receipt of gross income. No tax could have been more generally applied nor more easily computed. It simply took one cent out of every dollar that any resident of Indiana received from almost any source. The Adams Manufacturing Company challenged the statute on the ground that a tax on the receipts of its products manufactured in Indiana but sold in other states was violative of the commerce clause of the Constitution. The Supreme Court sustained this view. Justice Black, however, declaring that "taxation" and "regulation" were not synonymous, pointed out that it would be an unfair burden on intra-state commerce to force it to bear the entire tax burden while comparable interstate commerce escaped. To him this seemed to be the worst sort of discrimination and one that the Founders had not intended to sanction.

By the end of Black's first term as Associate Justice of the Supreme Court it was plain that by his appointment the President had indeed injected new blood into the Court. His professional competence was no longer open to question although the preconceived idea that he was not sufficiently learned in the intricacies of the law had died hard. As late as May 1938 Marquis Childs was still writing upon this assumption and reporting that Black was causing his colleagues on the Court "acute discomfort and embarrassment" because he was "unable to carry his share of the heavy burden of work that falls upon the Court." [36] Some astonished persons, admitting the strength of his opinions, suggested that perhaps he did not write them, and Washington rumor pointed to New Dealer Thomas Corcoran as the "ghost." In referring to those who reasoned thus Max Lerner said:

They cannot help admiring the courage and ability shown in his decisions; yet the censor that watches over our self-esteem will not permit them to confess that they were wrong about him in the first place. The result is the conclusion that since the opinions are good ones, it must have been a couple of other fellows who wrote them.[37]

Competent critics, however, were not long in realizing that Black's legal learning and ability were consistently above what had been expected. Robert Cushman, professor of Constitutional Law at Cornell University, was asked by a member of an audience he was addressing whether he regarded Justice Black as "the type of mind" fit for the Court. He replied that, although had he been in President Roosevelt's place he would not have made the appointment, he now believed the new Justice "much more able and intelligent than most people suppose." [38] Professor Walton Hamilton of the Yale Law School in an article of unstinted praise declared that "outside of the priesthood of the law, almost all men of substance and good will would accept his attitude as common sense";[39] and Professor Harold Havinghurst of the Northwestern School of Law wrote: "In the vernacular of the day, the Justice *has* something. And what he has is of great significance for the future of constitutional law and the nation." [40]

Two fairly distinct patterns seemed to emerge from Justice Black's first-term performance. First, he accorded to long-established precedent a minimum of respect and showed scant compunction in overruling it. Moreover, his method of destroying that part of it that he considered wrong was by one lethal blow.

He had no patience with that "canon of judicial craftsmanship" which required that such demolition be preceded by such a gradual weakening of the structure that its final collapse would occasion little surprise.

Secondly, he had shown a marked tendency to interpret narrowly the constitutional restraints upon the states and to allow them generous latitude in the management of their internal affairs. What underlay this inclination could be suspected, although not yet asserted upon the basis of proof.

CHAPTER VI

STATE AND NATION

Undoubtedly the most persistent question that has stalked the Supreme Court throughout its history is that of proper balance in the relationship between the federal government and its constituent States. This balance involves something more than the mere question of whether the state or federal government shall assume a particular function. For example, the method by which one of these governments performs a task admittedly within the scope of its authority may become objectionable to the other, and the settlement of such objections requires a resort to the doctrine of federalism even though there be no dispute as to whether the particular function is state or national. Older than the Supreme Court and coeval with the Union itself, the problem has survived the vicissitudes of war and the mutations of time and seems destined to demand attention so long as the government remains federal or the states retain any element of sovereignty. Therefore one of the inquiries usually made about the predilections of a new justice regards his anticipated reaction to this problem.

Yet this question, despite its age and notoriety, has readily lent itself to a deceptive simplification. Perhaps it is because everyone is assumed to understand the basic issue that almost nobody does. The confusion in which a study of the subject is too often approached seems to stem from a mental picture of two greedy and selfish powers, State and Nation, each jealous of its own preroga-

tives and ever fearful that the other may trespass upon its pre-
serves. Whatever degree of truth such concept may have presented
in the days of Marshall, it has now for a long time been an in-
accurate portrayal of the facts.

In almost all of the present-day litigation involving the rights
of a State it is not the federal government which seems offended
that the State is impinging upon its jurisdiction. When that cry is
raised it is by the person, natural or artificial, whose power the
State is attempting to curtail or whose operations it is undertaking
to regulate. Only infrequently does the federal government appear to have an adversary's interest in the matter. When the State
of Washington attempts to tax salesmen of a corporation domiciled in Delaware for the privilege of doing business in Washington,[1] it is not likely to be the federal government that protests
the possible burden upon interstate commerce. Perhaps it is able
to bear such indignity calmly because it is secure in the knowledge that its interests will be vigorously espoused by the taxed
corporation. Likewise when the federal government decides to
regulate wages and hours of work, it is not the State governments that press the argument that their sovereignty is being
assailed, but employers who are quick to perceive that the legislation springs from an insidious purpose on the part of the
national government to diminish the constitutional jurisdiction of
the states.

Additional light that may help to dispel some confusion would
result from a recognition of the fact that men who reach positions
on the Supreme Bench are never devotees of pure theory but are
practical persons whose judgment of a theory is determined by

how it works when put in practice. When Charles M. Wiltse chose as a book title, *John C. Calhoun, Nationalist*,[2] public attention was at once arrested, yet the author was able to justify his thesis that during his early career the man who beyond all others is regarded as the exponent of states' rights was urging policies that established federal power and entrenched federal prerogative. Perhaps this example may help to shatter the delusion that there has ever existed any potent political group seeking to make either states' rights or nationalism anything more than a means to an end. Most of the theory finally evolved has been from the stress and strain put upon our anatomy of government by rival contentions over immediate interests.

In the years just before Justice Black's appointment many persons in both political and academic circles seemed about to conclude that the long struggle between states' rights and federal potency had at long last ended in a virtual victory for the latter. There was much talk of the "obsolescence of federalism," and the "new centralization." "Regionalism" became a widely discussed topic, and both scholarly journals and popular periodicals carried articles which suggested various and elaborate plans for replacing the outmoded states with administrative *arrondissements*.

Many of those who rejoiced at what appeared to them to be the passing of the states were among the so-called liberals who approved Black's appointment. They believed that the states had become convenient tools of reactionary forces bent on retarding social progress and thought that whatever was done to limit state power would aid the national government in the advancement of its newly expanded program for social betterment. Therefore it was thought by some that Justice Black, himself a loyal supporter of the New Deal, could be counted on to exert his influence to increase the power of the national government at the expense of the states.

It was not long before it became apparent that the new Justice was pursuing no such general course. On the contrary, his opinions seemed to reflect a commitment to the proposition that the states retained under the Constitution exclusive control in certain fields of government. More consistently than any member of the Court he undertook to uphold the authority of the several states to levy taxes according to their chosen methods, to control business within their borders as their respective legislatures saw fit, and to regulate the rates and practices of their public service corporations with a minimum of interference from the federal government.

If votes and opinions dealing with such issues as these indicate a jealous regard for the preservation of the prerogatives of the states, is it to be said conversely and by the same token that he must be counted a strict constructionist where the federal government seeks to exercise its powers in a field theretofore reserved for state action? It was soon seen that neither his expressions nor his votes would justify that conclusion. On the contrary, he uniformly tends to favor liberal construction when federal authority is challenged. The direction of his thought in this regard is well illustrated by reference to his opinions relating to the scope and application of the federal labor statutes. He has been willing to hold that the Fair Labor Standards Act includes within its purview the work of many employees whose duties are but slightly and indirectly connected with interstate commerce, and he has consistently voted to sustain the orders and authority of the National Labor Relations Board. How he has reconciled these positions readily appears from an examination of cases and a rather consistent pattern of thought will be found woven into the fabric of his decisions.

When the Supreme Court has seen fit to invalidate state legislation it has commonly employed the commerce clause of the Constitution or the due process clause of the Fourteenth Amendment. Neither of these instruments has the practical drawback of definiteness, from which it results that a decision accomplished by their use is seldom so specific in expression as to furnish much clue as to how far its principle may be extended at some time in the future. But it is just this absence of a sharp cutting edge that makes them so handy, albeit quite as lethal in effect as the better defined constitutional limitations. In the field of constitutional interpretation the use of "blunt instruments" has certain advantages.

Thus any restrictive regulation of business to some extent affects commerce, and the least departure from procedural propriety verges toward a denial of due process, so that the Court's concern has been to determine what degree of interference or denial shall be sufficient to be considered interference or denial at all, a situation necessarily leaving much to be measured by " the length of the chancellor's foot." The fact that a state has been halted from fixing the price of gasoline[3] is no warrant for saying that it may not fix the price of milk,[4] nor is its right to dispense with the formality of a common law indictment[5] any indication that it may get by with a trial wherein the accused lacks the benefit of counsel,[6] a right of far fresher origin than that involving the necessity of an indictment.

Justice Black seems disinclined to employ these indefinite criteria in cases wherein the right of a state to regulate business within its borders is questioned. He has consistently argued that in the absence of congressional legislation a state possesses the power to tax the operation of a business even though such operation is a part of interstate commerce. The application of the due process clause he would almost confine to the protection of personal liberty.

A case illustrative of Black's disinclination to allow the commerce clause to prevent a state from imposing taxes as it saw fit, was Gwin, White and Prince v. Henneford.[7] Here the Court was called upon to determine whether a Washington tax on gross receipts was invalid as an interference with interstate commerce when applied to a fruit marketer which shipped the greater part of its fruit to points of sale in other states and foreign countries. Justice Stone for the Court held that the tax, although applied only to persons receiving funds in the State of Washington, discriminated in its practical operation against interstate commerce by imposing upon it the risk of multiple taxation to which local commerce was not exposed. He could forsee that "such a multiplication of State taxes, each measured by the volume of the commerce, would re-establish the barriers to interstate trade which it was the object of the commerce clause to remove."[8]

Justice Black, on the other hand, felt that the Supreme Court, by deciding that such a tax could not be applied to one who obtained his receipts by engaging in interstate commerce, laid an unjust burden upon intrastate business by forcing it to bear the entire burden of state taxation. Thus, intrastate commerce, he said, will pay its way; interstate commerce will not. But suppose, as the majority seemed to fear, two states should tax the same business. Black could see no intrinsic harm in that. It was only fair, he thought, that a business which was operating in two or more states should bear its part of the tax burden of each. Moreover, if this multiple taxation did prove unjust Congress was authorized to remedy the resulting evils, and was the only arm of the government that did have such authority.

Upon the same reasoning he joined in a dissenting opinion by Justice Douglas in the case of McLeod *v.* Dilworth Company.[9] This time the Court had held that Arkansas had no power to exact a sales tax from a Tennessee firm which shipped large quantities of machinery to Arkansas. Justice Frankfurter, speaking for the Court, declared that the tax involved an assumption of power by Arkansas which the commerce clause plainly forbade. Admitting that a use tax might have been valid, and that a sales tax and a use tax often accomplished the same results,[10] he nevertheless concluded that they were different "in conception." The dissenters had little patience with such a fine-spun distinction and declared that since a sales tax and a use tax had exactly the same economic effect it was useless to quibble over differences "in conception." They would have upheld the Arkansas tax and they strongly disapproved of the Court's opinion which, they thought, placed local industry at a competitive disadvantage with interstate trade.[11]

Nor has Justice Black been any more tolerant of the use of the due process clause than of the commerce clause as a restriction upon the power of the states to regulate business. A dissent from a *per curiam* opinion in the case of Polk Company v. Glover[12] shows him voting to uphold a Florida statute which required that all containers used for fruit produced in Florida should have stamped upon them the name of the state. Insisting that the Florida legislators were peculiarly qualified to determine the policies that related to one of their state's greatest industries, he placed considerable emphasis on the fact that the statute had passed the Florida Senate by a vote of 24 to 1 and the House by a vote of 70 to 0, failing to say, however, why the proportion of votes by which a measure was passed should be considered in determining its validity.

On somewhat similar reasoning he would have upheld the validity of an Arizona statute limiting the number of cars a train could carry in that state.[13] The majority of the Court held that the restriction had no reasonable relation to safety and for that reason could not be defended as a valid exercise of the police power. Thus they concluded it was unconstitutional in that it deprived the railroads of their liberty and property without due process of law. Justice Black regarded this decision as an attempt on the part of the Court to substitute its judgment as to the wisdom of the statute for that of the state legislature and in dissent said, "What the Court decides today is that it was unwise governmental policy to regulate the length of trains,"[14] a single statement in which his whole argument is eloquently implicit.

Not susceptible to such wide extension as the commerce and due process clauses, yet sometimes the basis for an attack upon state legislation is the constitutional prohibition against state enactments impairing the obligations of contracts. Justice Black has shown no disposition to render more respect to this provision than to the commerce and due process clauses when it is invoked to condemn legislation which may incidentally affect rights arising from existing agreements. Early in his career he had exhibited this tendency in the teacher tenure case[15] and later he took the same position in the case of Wood v. Lovett.[16]

In 1935 Arkansas had passed a statute which provided that when land was sold by the state for non-payment of taxes, the sale could not afterwards be set aside because of any irregularity in the assessment of the property. In 1936 the state sold certain lands it had acquired in 1933 because of non-payment of taxes. In 1937 the 1935 act was repealed and in 1939 a corporation which had owned the land before it was confiscated for non-payment of taxes brought suit to cancel the state's deed on the ground that prior to the sale there were irregularities which rendered the proceeding void. The purchasers of the land who had bought it while the law of 1935 was in force contended that if the 1937 act should be held to divest them of title confirmed by the act of 1935, it would constitute an impairment of the obligation of their contracts with the state.

This contention the Court upheld upon the rule that laws which subsist at the time and place a contract is made become a part of its terms. Searching into the history of the statute, Justice Black in a dissenting opinion concluded that the legislature in 1937 repealed the 1935 statute because it had become convinced that the law had worked counter to the state's policy of promoting continuity of possession by home owners and farmers. Depending upon the reasoning of the Court in the Minnesota moratorium case[17] which he thought indicated "a realistic appreciation of the fact that ours is an evolving society and that general words of the contract clause were not intended to reduce the legislative branch of the government to helpless impotency," [18] he argued that there was no obligation on the part of Arkansas to retain forever its general law concerning forfeiture of property and the sale of land. The state had not promised the purchasers, he said, that it would keep on its statute books legislation affecting forfeited lands directly opposed to what had been the Arkansas law at the time of the forfeiture. The contract clause could not be stretched far enough to imply any such obligation.

Justice Black's latitudinarian attitude toward the exercise of state power employed to effect social and economic ends abates considerably when the experiment is in the field of politics. Although he has no ear for the Florida fruit packer who thinks his state makes unreasonable regulations about how he shall label his product, nor for the railroad that complains about Arizona's prohibition of long freight trains, he is at once alert when some citizen reports that his voting franchise has been abridged or its influence diluted by arbitrary state legislation. Despite his sharp criticism of opinions striking down state statutes in other cases he has not hesitated to place his stamp of disapproval upon electoral devices which operate to give unequal value to votes according to the location of the voter.

In such a case involving an Illinois statute he joined Justice Douglas in dissent from a *per curiam* opinion.[19] The statute provided that in order for a new political party to obtain for its candidates a place on the ballot a petition had to be presented bearing the signatures of twenty-five thousand voters, including two hundred signatures from each of fifty of the state's one-hundred-and-two counties. When the Progressive Party failed to get two hundred signatures from fifty separate counties its members protested that the requirement that it do so constituted a denial of due process and a violation of the equal protection and privileges and immunities clauses of the Fourteenth Amendment. Pointing out that 52 per cent of Illinois voters resided in Cook County alone, and that 87 per cent were residents of the forty-nine most populous counties, they demonstrated that the challenged legislative act made it possible for a new party's lack of favor in the less populous counties to exclude the names of its candidates from the ballot even though they should be the choice of a large majority of the state's voters.

The majority of the Court was not impressed that this possibility reflected an unconstitutional discrimination. The Constitution itself, they said, provided for unequal representation to populations and it would be "strange indeed and doctrinaire" to deny to a state power to do likewise. Justices Douglas, Black, and Murphy, however, thought that the statute did discriminate unconstitutionally by conferring upon the voters of the rural counties a power not possessed by those of the metropolitan areas.

Likewise, in company with Justice Douglas, Justice Black dissented from another *per curiam* opinion refusing to interfere with Georgia's carefully contrived "county unit system" by which the state sees to it that "city slickers" and colored people shall not by their preponderating numbers have the power to select state officials and members of Congress.[20] Under this system which allocates votes to counties rather than men, allowing no county more than six votes and every county as many as one, it was demonstrated that a citizen's vote in a rural county could be one-hundred-and-twenty times as influential as that of another citizen who happened to live in Atlanta and that on a statewide average each vote outside the limits of Fulton County had eleven times the weight of the Fulton County resident's ballot. To Douglas and Black this seemed an insult to democracy and contemptuous of the Fourteenth Amendment, as well as violative of the constitutional provision that members of both houses of Congress shall be chosen by the people. "The creation by law of favored groups of citizens and the grant to them of preferred political rights" they held to be "the worst of all discriminations under a democratic system of government."[21] The dissenting opinion suggested that the American voter in order to be protected against discrimination ought not to have to be a Negro, Catholic, or Jew, somewhat remindful of the ancient plaint,

> I wish I were an Indian, a Choctaw or a Ute,
> And not a common white man, an unprotected brute.

It was the opinion of the dissenters that because voters could not be discriminated against because of their race or religion it did not follow that they could be on account of their urbanity or geographical residence.

Justice Black's determination to prevent the Court from blocking legislation has not faltered when the legislation has been that of the federal government rather than that of the states. His conviction that the Court should allow the greatest possible freedom to legislative bodies in matters of economic and social legislation applies equally to both state and federal governments. Thus, not only Congress, but most of the quasi-legislative agencies of the national government have found in him a defender of their actions.[22] Perhaps cases involving rulings of the National Labor Relations Board best illustrate his attitude.

In 1939 the case of National Labor Relations Board v. Fansteel Metallurgical Corporation[23] presented to the Court the question of the Board's authority to require the re-employment of persons discharged for engaging in a sit-down strike. There was but little question that the company had been guilty of unfair labor practices as defined in the National Labor Relations Act and that in retaliation the employees had seized the plant and held it until ejected by the police. The Board found that the unlawful conduct of the employer had led to the strike and concluded that the striking employees were protected by the provisions of the act which provided for the reinstatement of those who strike because of unfair labor practices.

The company, desiring not to re-employ certain workers who had seized its property and held it unlawfully, appealed to the courts from the Board's order that such employees be reinstated. When the case finally reached the Supreme Court Chief Justice Hughes, speaking for a seven-man majority, declared that it was not the purpose of the National Labor Relations Act to force an employer to retain in his service those who had illegally seized and held his property. The fact that the employer had been guilty of

97

unfair practices, the Chief Justice pointed out, did not deprive it of its legal rights to possess and protect its property, and although the employees did have a right to strike, they did not have a right to commit acts of violence. To justify such conduct, he thought, "would be to put a premium on resort to force instead of legal remedies." [24]

Justice Reed who wrote the dissent and Justice Black who concurred thought the Board was within its rights in ordering the reinstatement of the workers and said:

> It is the function of the Board to weigh the charges and countercharges and determine the adjustment most conducive to industrial peace. Courts certainly should not interfere with the normal action of administrative bodies in such circumstances.[25]

If the strikers had acted unlawfully, continued the dissenters, appropriate punishment should be meted out by the law-enforcing agency of the state and not by a United States district court's denial to them of the protection of the National Labor Relations Act.[26]

A somewhat similar case involved seamen who had gone on strike while their ship was in some port other than the home port and had subsequently been discharged by the steamship company by which they were employed. The National Labor Relations Board ordered the company to reinstate them and the company thereupon appealed to the Court which held that since the seamen had been guilty of the criminal offense of mutiny the Board was not authorized to require their reinstatement.[27] Again Justices Black and Reed dissented, declaring that the unlawful conduct of a strike provoked by unfair practices of the employer does not have the effect of withdrawing from the Board its power to reinstate the strikers if it sees fit to do so.[28]

The Federal Trade Commission and the Federal Power Commission, both of which agencies have followed courses quite in accord with Black's own political and economic views, have likewise seen their rulings consistently supported by Justice Black.[29] The Interstate Commerce Commission, on the other hand, has several times incurred his severe denunciation, a fact that engenders some doubt as to his devotion to the theory of judicial restraint that he has so often urged his brethren to use in reviewing the work of other administrative agencies.

An example is furnished in a case involving an order of the Interstate Commerce Commission that permitted railroads running out of Chicago to charge higher rates on grain shipments that had come part of the way by barge than on those that had made the whole journey by rail.[30] The majority of the Court sustained the Commission in permitting the differential, but Justice Black dissented and criticized the Commission for approving a rate revision which patently was intended to force shippers to use railroads instead of barge lines. The Commission, he declared, had failed to carry out a plain declaration of policy as announced by Congress, that of providing fair and impartial regulation of all modes of transportation.[31]

In the case of Interstate Commerce Commission v. Parker[32] his suspicion of the Commission again showed itself. Here the Commission had granted to a railroad a certificate of public convenience and necessity for motor truck operation. The fact that the territory was already served by a motor carrier and that there was no evidence that its service was inadequate was given little consideration. Nevertheless the majority of the Court upheld the Commission's order. Justices Douglas and Black dissented, making no secret of the fact that they considered the Commission railroad-minded, and charging that it construed the term "convenience and necessity" found in the Commerce Act to mean the railroad's convenience and necessity rather than that of the public. "Would it be thought for a moment," they asked, "that motor carriers could obtain authority to build a new competing railroad by any such standard of 'motor carrier convenience.'" [33]

It is by no means to be supposed that Justice Black has never voted to uphold orders of the Interstate Commerce Commission, but it is apparent from a review of the cases that he has accorded it a far less favorable consideration than he has given other federal regulatory bodies. It is likewise worthy of note that each time the Justice has been opposed to upholding one of the Commission's orders, it has been a situation in which he considered that it had dealt unfairly with the interest of the public rather than with the interest of a carrier. [34]

One further indication of Justice Black's sympathy with federal regulation remains to be noted. It is his consistent readiness to extend the term "commerce" to matters which had formerly been assumed to be beyond its meaning thereby greatly augmenting the scope of the federal regulatory authority. For example, when a majority of the Court in the case of McLeod v. Threlkeld[35] decided that a cook who prepared and served meals to maintenance of way employees of an interstate railroad was not engaged in commerce and hence outside the scope of the Fair Labor Standards Act, Black joined a dissent which declared him within the operation of the act. Likewise he disagreed when the Court decided that maintenance employees of an office building that leased offices to firms engaged in interstate commerce and to those engaged purely in intrastate commerce were not covered by the act.[36]

When the Court found that the Western Union Telegraph Company was not prohibited by the Fair Labor Standards Act from employing child labor since it was not a "producer" and did not "ship" messages in interstate commerce,[37] Black protested that the niceties of semantics should not require the sacrifice of social gains. He and Justice Murphy who wrote the dissent could see no valid reason for holding that the telegraph company was not engaged in interstate commerce.

Not only in cases involving the Fair Labor Standards Act has Justice Black striven to broaden the interpretation of the term commerce. The outstanding example of this disposition was in connection with insurance policies which the Court seventy-five years before had said were not "commodities to be shipped or forwarded from one state to another." [38] Exhibiting once more his total lack of compunction in unsettling long established holdings, Black declared that the sale of insurance policies *did* constitute commerce and thereby subjected the insurance business to federal regulation.[39]

In the few cases where the Federal government and the states have actually appeared as adversary parties it cannot be said that Justice Black has revealed any fixed sympathy with one sovereign as against the other. In New York *v.* United States[40] he stuck with Marshall's view that the power to tax should not by implication be conceded to one sovereignty as against the other. Here the United States sought to tax the business of bottling mineral water even though the business was conducted by the state of New York. Justice Frankfurter, speaking for the Court, reasoned that a state by engaging in a trading business could not withdraw that business from the power of Congress to tax any more than it could by state ownership of a transport agency remove it from the regulatory powers of the Federal government acquired under the commerce clause of the Constitution. He spoke lightly of Marshall's warning that the power to tax is the power to destroy as a sort of outmoded dictum that had died of old age and a changing climate finally to be buried under an appropriate epitaph by Justice Holmes.

Justice Douglas in a dissenting opinion in which Justice Black concurred strongly criticized such reasoning. It was inconsistent with the idea of separate sovereignty, he declared, that one government can tax another without the latter's express consent and a step toward relegating the states " to a more servile status."

However, in the cases involving the title to tidelands against a state's sea coast Justice Black with the Court's majority voted to sustain the claims of the Federal government against California, Louisiana, and Texas.[41]

What, then, can be said concerning Justice Black's stand on the problem of federalism? The truth of the matter seems to be that he is far less concerned with the theory of federalism than the language he adopts might indicate, and less concerned perhaps than he himself recognizes. He speaks in lofty terms of a judicial policy protecting the pristine rights of the states, but does not allow such a view to stand in the way permitting the federal government a free hand in the regulation of labor conditions within the states. On the other hand, no other member of the Court has seemed so concerned with protecting the rights of the states to regulate business within their borders. He declaims fervently for allowing federal administrative agencies free rein, but once let such an agency digress from his standards of rightness, and this tendency is found to be less influential than his desires for what he considers a proper result.

There is little question of the sincerity of his concern with social improvement and human betterment, and he is firm in his faith that these ends can be best accomplished by an active government. Hence, when he conceives that a government, be it state or national, is attempting to employ its powers to benefit its population, he is anxious that it be allowed to proceed. Government, he believes, has a duty to use its power positively and actively to protect the weak from the power of the strong, the rights of the little from the ambitions of the big, the possessions of the poor from the rapacity of the rich. He is the little man's advocate upon the Court, and if it is sometimes necessary to sacrifice theoretical consistency to protect his client's immediate interest, he is not unwilling to make the sacrifice. Whether or not this conclusion is justified may more clearly appear from an examination of his votes and expressions upon a group of miscellaneous cases where about the only element common to all is the thread of the common man's interest, mediate or immediate, in the outcome of the contest.

CHAPTER VII

LITTLE MAN'S ADVOCATE

If there yet remains an element of truth in the complaint that "laws grind the poor and rich men rule the law," it is not the fault of Justice Black. On the contrary, his sympathy consistently appears to be with the weaker of two unequal adversaries and often glows through the text of his opinions. In labor disputes he is generally on the side of the employee, and readily grants to labor legislation that liberality of interpretation to which remedial legislation is said to be entitled. In personal damage suits the plaintiff finds in him a friend at court, particularly where the legal relationship of master and servant exists, for he is bitter in his denunciation of such doctrines as "the assumption of risk" and of such devices as the directed verdict which commonly work to the disadvantage of the plaintiff.

Such a statement warrants an examination of the shield's reverse side, for admittedly some signs may be found to indicate that the Justice's propensity to protect the poor is corollary to a distrust of the rich. Yet there are scarcely enough such clues to outline a dependable pattern because cases are few in which wealth and power are assailed wholly apart from the interests of the less privileged. Since so often the same result may follow from being pro-poor man as from being anti-rich man, it is not easy to pursue an analysis to the primary predilection.

There are, however, some cases involving powerful interests,

104

such as those concerning the enforcement of the anti-trust laws and patent infringement, in which the little man is not a litigant, and in these too Justice Black has displayed a rather antagonistic turn of mind toward big business. Certainly he is impervious to the suggestion implicit in so much conservative thought, that what has grown so big and powerful must have grown so by the performance of some valuable public service. Even in these cases it may be argued that Justice Black is thinking in terms of the consumer of goods as an interested party, so that the shadow of the little man still falls across the controversy. At any rate this much may be safely said, that whatever its remote or spiritual source, the fact is that Justice Black is entitled to be called the little man's advocate and has shown a willing disposition to sweep aside technical distinctions where they appear to work to the advantage of the rich and powerful. In support of this view it is well enough to begin with the examination of cases involving the interests of labor, keeping in mind, however, that they represent but one facet of a single stone.

A serious threat to the success of organized labor during its period of adolescence was a tendency on the part of the federal courts to declare certain of the activities of trade unions to be in restraint of trade and hence illegal under the Sherman Act. It was to remove labor organizations from the operation of this act that the Clayton Act was passed. Although at the time of its passage this statute was hailed as "Labor's Magna Carta," it failed to settle finally the question of whether certain specific union activities as secondary boycotts were within the prohibition of the Sherman Act. It was this question that presented itself in the case of Milk Wagon Drivers Union *v.* Lake Valley Company.[1] The dispute had arisen as a result of the vendor system whereby independent dealers bought milk from dairies and from their own vehicles distributed it to retailers. When these vendors refused to abide by the standards that the organized milk wagon drivers had set up, the union drivers picketed the stores which the vendors supplied, alleging that they were unfair to union labor. Upon the complaint of the retailers and the vendors a United States district court issued an injunction prohibiting such picketing, holding that there was no labor dispute within the meaning of the Norris-LaGuardia Act and that the picketing constituted a secondary boycott in violation of the Sherman Act.

With such reasoning, Justice Black, writing the opinion of the Court, sharply disagreed. Congress had made it quite clear, he said, that what was regarded as a judicial misinterpretation of the Clayton Act should not be repeated in construing the Norris-LaGuardia Act, and any court that granted an injunction in a case growing out of a labor dispute where no more than some alleged violation of the Sherman Act was involved, was directly contravening the declared purpose of Congress.

In the case of Hunt *v.* Crumboch[2] he again rejected the theory that laboring men were guilty of an infringement of the anti-trust laws by joining in a common purpose to refuse to work for a certain firm. A motor carrier that hauled for the Atlantic and Pacific Tea Company had refused to unionize its business and had continued to operate while a strike was being carried on by organized truck drivers. When the Atlantic and Pacific Tea Company finally entered into a closed shop agreement with the union and notified all haulers of merchandise that they must become union members in order to enjoy the firm's patronage, the carrier that had operated during the strike found that the union would not negotiate with it nor admit any of its employees to union membership. The result was that the Atlantic and Pacific Tea Company under the terms of its closed shop agreement could not continue to do business with the carrier. The same situation prevented the carrier from obtaining other contracts and in this predicament it appealed to the courts.

Justice Black saw the question as this: Does the Sherman Act prohibit laboring men from refusing to admit to union membership employees of particular persons and from refusing to sell their services to these persons? He answered in the negative holding laborers free to sell their labor to whom they please and not required to sell it to those with whom for any reason they are displeased.

Justices Roberts, Stone, Frankfurter and Jackson dissented on the ground that since the sole purpose of the union was to destroy the business of the carrier and not to improve the condition of the workers, the differences between the litigants should not be regarded as a labor controversy. It followed, they thought, that the purpose and action of the workers who refused to be employed by the carrier constituted a conspiracy that the Sherman Act forbade in that it lessened competition in commerce.[3]

Yet notwithstanding Black's attitude where labor unions were charged with violation of the anti-trust laws, his sympathy quickly waned when he came to consider the case of union members who had combined with their employers in a common purpose to restrain trade. This was the factual basis of the suit of Allen Bradley Company *v.* Local Union No. 3, International Brotherhood of Electrical Workers.[4] Some of the members of the brotherhood were employed by manufacturers in the production of electrical equipment and other members were employed by contractors who installed such equipment. The members who installed equipment refused to work for contractors who did not buy from manufacturers who employed members of the local union and the manufacturing members of the union, in turn, refused to work for manufacturers who sold their products to contractors who did not use union labor. This was one union policy that apparently appealed to the employers. At any rate, it was readily accepted by both the contractors and the manufacturers, and the combination of the three—union, contractors, and manufacturers—all working to a common end, presented a picture to warm the hearts of those who preach that the interests of labor and capital are identical.

The business of the local manufacturers throve and prospered. Since contractors under the agreement were not free to buy from outside producers, the inside producers were relieved of troublesome competition and were able to increase their prices until they were selling goods within the New York City area at prices considerably higher than they sold the identical goods elsewhere. Also the contractors were satisfied. Although they had to pay high prices for the equipment they passed the charges on to the consumer with no fear that he would be able to employ other contractors. The result was that interstate sale of electrical equipment in the New York area was almost entirely suppressed. Behold how good and how pleasant it was for brethren to dwell together in unity!

Justice Black was unimpressed by this example of concord between labor and management. Admitting that if the labor union had acted by itself to effect such a situation there would have been no violation of the Sherman Act, he thought the fact that the employers were parties to the same scheme and benefitted by its operation brought it within the prohibition of the act.[5] Just why a situation created entirely by labor without the aid of others would be any less obnoxious and burdensome to the consumer is not easy to understand, but the Court was merely construing a statute and the fact that the employers were partners in the scheme seemed to bring it within the purview of the law.

It is not to be denied, however, that there are cases in which unions acting alone have incurred Black's disapproval. In instances where organized labor has seemed to him to be manifestly working to the disadvantage of the public he has not hesitated to speak and vote against it. John L. Lewis and Caesar Petrillo are two labor leaders who have on occasion lost Black's support by their high-handed methods. When Lewis and his miners, relying upon the Norris-LaGuardia Anti-injunction Act, failed to obey a mandate of a district court forbidding them to terminate an agreement with the government, Black agreed with the Court that prohibitions of the anti-injunction act were not applicable to the sovereign and hence did not preclude the government from obtaining an injunction.[6] Even so he thought that the fines imposed upon Lewis and the union were excessive and that they should have been conditioned upon the failure of the defendants to comply with the Court's order by a future date.

With Petrillo Black showed less sympathy. By forbidding union members to perform for broadcasting stations that did not employ a certain number of union members, Petrillo had successfully intimidated broadcasters into hiring more musicians than they wanted or needed. To restrain this practice of "feather-bedding" Congress enacted the Lea Act forbidding any person to coerce a broadcasting station to employ "any person or persons in excess of the number of employees needed." This act, Petrillo charged, was repugnant to the due process clause of the Fifth Amendment because the phrase "number of employees needed" was so vague and uncertain that ordinary men could not determine whether a contemplated action would fall within the law's denunciation.[7] Speaking for the Court Justice Black answered with sarcasm that there might be clearer and more precise language than that Congress had used but that he could not think of any.

Although he generally approves the activities of labor unions, Black's sympathy is by no means limited to that segment of labor which has seen fit to organize. It is the laboring man and not the labor union with which he is primarily concerned. While he is ready to uphold the union so long as it seems to be working to the advantage of the laborer, he has sanctioned over bitter union protest state legislation designed to protect the independent worker.

Certain states, either by statute or constitutional amendment, have outlawed closed shop agreements and provided that no worker shall be discriminated against because he is or is not a member of a labor organization. When the unions challenged such legislation on the grounds that it deprived their members of equal protection of the law and due process of law as guaranteed by the Fourteenth Amendment, Black wrote the opinion of the Court upholding the legislation.[8] Pointing out that the Court had upheld state statutes forbidding employers to discriminate against union members, he thought it logically followed that it must approve statutes forbidding discrimination against non-union workers. The Constitutional rights of organized laboring men, he said, did not include a guarantee that none but themselves should get and hold jobs.

The right of laboring men to put their cause before the public has been consistently upheld by Justice Black. Neither attendant circumstances of violence and bloodshed nor the comprehensive authority of a state to exercise its police power has seemed to him any reason to restrict the right of labor to publish its grievances by means of pickets so long as the picketing is not being employed to accomplish purposes clearly violative of valid state legislation. In the case of Milk Wagon Drivers Union *v.* Meadowbrook Dairies[9] he declined to agree with the Court that the "clear and present danger test" sufficed to justify an injunction against peaceful picketing because, "the momentum of fear generated by past violence would survive even though future picketing might be wholly peaceful." [10] It was going too far, he thought, to deny six thouasnd members of a union the right to express their opinion through the medium of the picket line in an effort to end the effect of fear generated by the lawless acts of a few individuals.

Where, however, the picketing has been utilized to bring about the violation of state law Black has refused to sanction it. Thus when Kansas City ice peddlers sought by picketing to persuade

111

HUGO L. BLACK

an ice manufacturer to sell only to union members in violation of a Missouri anti-trade restraint law he spoke for the Court in holding that an injunction could properly issue against such union activity.[11] The Constitutional guaranty of freedom of speech, he said, does not extend to speech or writing designed to force violation of a valid criminal statute.

On the other hand, however, he was unwilling to allow the Illinois anti-trust law to be made the basis for permitting a state court injunction to restrict the use of picket lines to a particular locality where the labor dispute originated. Here he dissented from an opinion written by Justice Frankfurter which had held that members of building trade unions should not be allowed to picket the restaurant of a man who was having no labor trouble at that place.[12] The owner of the restaurant had employed a contractor to construct a building for him a mile and a half distant from the restaurant and wholly unconnected with it. According to the terms of the contract, the contractor reserved the right to make his own arrangements regarding the employment of labor in the construction. He employed non-union carpenters and because of this the organized carpenters proceeded to picket his employer's cafe, declaring the owner to be unfair to organized labor.

The state court held that the union thereby violated the state's anti-trust law and enjoined the carpenter's union from picketing in front of the cafe. A majority of five members of the Supreme Court upheld this determination on the ground that the state was entitled to exercise its police power to protect the public interest as it saw fit. Justice Black, on the contrary, considered the action of the state court a clear violation of the freedom of speech guaranteed by the Fourteenth Amendment.

112

Similarly he dissented from an opinion of the Court which upheld an injunction against the picketing of a self-employer's place of business in an attempt to coerce him to adopt a union shop.[13] Here it should be noted there was no state statute specifically forbidding such union activity.

A case of slight significance in itself, yet typical of Black's predisposition in favor of the working man, involved tips given to Redcaps.[14] A railroad terminal company had contracted with the Redcaps who worked for it that their tips should be reported to the company and the amount deducted from their wages. The result was that the company itself would not have to pay the entire amount required by the Fair Labor Standards Act. The question boiled down to whether tips could be considered wages under the terms of the act, and the majority of the Court answered that they could. The odor of deception was too strong to permit Black's concurrence. He said:

One who gives a redcap a tip does not necessarily know that he is thereby helping the railroad to discharge its statutory duty of paying a minimum wage to its employees. The tip-paying public is entitled to know whom it tips, the redcap or the railroad. A plan like that before us, which covertly diverts the tips from employees for whom the giver intended them to employers for whom the giver did not intend them and to whom any kind of gift doubtless would not have been voluntarily given, seems to me to contain an element of deception.[15]

From the foregoing cases it appears that Justice Black's leaning toward the laborer's side of judicial controversies does not result from a conviction that civilization's development has reached a point where the dominance of a new social class is demanded, but from no more than the fact that labor's side is so often also the side of the little litigant as opposed to the big one. Where this coincidence fails and labor becomes the Goliath as in the case of the United Mine Workers or the American Federation of Musicians, Black does not hesitate to espouse the cause of its adversary.

From this premise of Justice Black's concern to protect the interests of the little man it would not have been difficult to predict how he would stand on the matter of directed verdicts, a judicial device used so often to the advantage of defendants in personal damage suits that even the *Encyclopedia Britannica* has noted that characteristic as its most distinguishing.[16] It is one thing to mumble the maxim that is supposed to mark the boundary between the respective functions of judge and jury,[17] but quite another to lay out the fine line that divides issues of fact from those of law. It is the uncertain marking of this borderline that generates the multitude of cases in which appellate courts are called on to say whether a trial judge has exceeded his authority in withdrawing an issue from the jury or in peremptorily ordering it decided in a particular way. It is unlikely that any other question of trial practice has engaged so much attention from superior courts.[18]

Assuredly it is a proper principle of pure law to require that allegations be supported by proof or else discarded in the consideration of the case. From this it follows that a litigant onerated with the burden of proof must lose his case if he is able to produce no evidence whatever to support some essential fact upon which it rests, and since in the absence of evidence there is nothing for the triers of fact to consider, he loses it as a matter of law, which is to say that he loses it by the judge's determination of the issue.

114

Just as certainly it must be a proper principle that where evidence upon material facts is so conflicting and of such quality that reasonable men may well differ as to what should be accepted as true or rejected as false, the issue is one for the jury. But between these plain examples there is a vast field over which speculative reasoning has spun a fine web in which even the most meticulous judicial logicians are often entangled.

When, for instance, is it to be said that there is no evidence of a disputed fact? Is it when there is not even a "scintilla" of such evidence, or is it when there is no "substantial" amount? Respectable courts have answered this question both ways.[19] If a scintilla is enough to take a case to the jury, just what is a scintilla, and since it is sometimes said to be sufficient if there is enough evidence to warrant a "legitimate inference," what is meant by legitimate inference as opposed to mere speculation, and by whose standards is the legitimacy of an inference determined? All these questions and scores of related ones have long engaged the attention of common-law jurists.

Added to the inherent complexity of the matter is the trait of human nature that drives judges as well as other persons in authority gradually to extend their range of prerogative. The use of the directed verdict is but one of many devices which have been adopted from time to time to remedy an obvious weakness of the jury system. The difficulty is that the remedy is sometimes worse than the disease it is intended to cure.

It is plausibly argued that if a trial judge knows from the paucity of evidence that he could not allow a verdict to stand upon it, he should be allowed to save the time of both court and

115

litigants by directing the jury to reach such a verdict as the law requires. This reasoning begets departure from the so-called "scintilla rule" which requires that so long as there is even very little evidence to support a contention any directed verdict against it must be regarded as an interference with the fact-finding function vested exclusively in the jury.[20] The extent to which departure from this rule could finally evolve has often given pause to those who are concerned with the preservation of trial by jury.

One legal philosopher so concerned is Justice Black, hailing from a state that has tenaciously held to the strictness of the old rule.[21] More likely than that his early training greatly influences him in this regard, however, is the fact that in many cases in which a trial is ended by a directed verdict some powerful party charged with the negligent injury of a plaintiff profits by the application of the judge's right to withdraw the issues from the jury. Black regards the directed verdict as but the latest in a long list of technics invented to circumscribe a litigant's right to "the judgment of his peers," and would consign it to the legal graveyard alongside the procedures of afforcement, attaint, and the other methods that courts have from time to time employed to hold rein upon the "passion, prejudice, and unaccountable caprice" to which juries are sometimes subject.

Probably the best index to the views of Justice Black upon directed verdicts is to be found in his dissenting opinion in the case of Galloway *v.* United States.[22] Here the petitioner sought benefits of war-risk insurance for total and permanent disability because of insanity which he claimed existed in 1919 at the time his policy lapsed for non-payment of premiums. His suit had been filed in 1938 so that it was necessary for him to show, not only that his disability existed, but had continuously existed for nineteen years. At the close of all the evidence the district judge sustained the government's motion for a directed verdict. The Circuit Court of Appeals affirmed the judgment, which the petitioner contended deprived him of trial by jury contrary to the provision of the Seventh Amendment.

In an opinion by Justice Rutledge the Supreme Court agreed with the lower courts that there was no evidence that the petitioner's disability had been continuous. Admittedly at the time of the trial he was insane and there was evidence that such had been his condition during the first World War. But, said the Court, there was lacking evidence of insanity during a period of eight years. Nothing in the Seventh Amendment, the opinion continued, obviates the necessity for some proof of every essential fact required to make out a plaintiff's case and the guaranty there embodied demands no more than that the jury be allowed to make reasonable inferences from fact proven in evidence.

Justice Black, with the concurrence of Justices Murphy and Douglas, dissented. Had the dissenters been content to differ with the majority merely upon the question of whether there was some substantial evidence that might have warranted a conclusion that petitioner's insanity had been continuous, their disagreement with their brethren would have been of little consequence. They were, however, unwilling to rest their objection on any such halfway ground and boldly assailed the whole judicial theory upon which the practice of directed verdicts is supported. The invention of directed verdicts, Black declared, was "a long step toward the determination of facts by judges instead of by juries," [23] and the fact that the Supreme Court had permitted it for ninety years seemed to him no reason why it should tolerate it any longer.

Perhaps in no other opinion has Justice Black exhibited such a passionate attachment to the grass-roots principles of pure democracy as in this case where there was involved no vestige of any current economic issue that might have influenced his purpose. He simply believed without reservation that factual disputes between citizens were better settled by the judgment of their peers than by judges, and he was tenaciously holding to that ancient doctrine in the face of current judicial philosophy. He seemed almost to charge the existence of a magisterial conspiracy to whittle away piece by piece the substance of the Seventh Amendment. The old rule that required submission of a litigant's case to a jury when there was any supporting evidence whatsoever had been given "an ugly name," he said—"the scintilla rule"—for the very purpose of discrediting it.

This rule, he conceded had been "completely repudiated" by the Court in 1872[24] and its traces systematically eradicated. As late as 1929, he pointed out, the Court had announced that a "judge might weigh the evidence to determine whether he, and not the jury, thought it was 'overwhelming' for either party and then direct a verdict." [25] Such reasoning, said Black, was wrong and in defiance of the plain meaning of the Seventh Amendment. Hence it should no longer be adhered to. Significant of his feeling on the matter of the right to trial by jury was the addition of a note to his dissent, affixed lest the reader mistakenly assume by reason of his exclusive discussion of the directed verdict that he looked with more tolerance upon other devices for judicial domination of juries. "I do not mean to minimize," he said, "other forms of judicial control." [26]

Another majority opinion which for like reason evoked a vigorous dissent from Justice Black was rendered in the case of Brady *v*. Southern Railroad Company.[27] Here the Court reviewed the propriety of submitting to a jury the question of a defendant's negligence. The North Carolina Supreme Court had decided that the case was improperly submitted to the jury and had reversed the judgment of the trial court. The United States Supreme Court agreed with this view.

The plaintiff's decedent had lost his life in a railroad accident because someone left a derailing device closed when it should have been open. The majority of the Court thought it speculative as to whether the deceased or some other employee of the railroad closed the derailer and concluded that the jury had guessed, without the aid of proved circumstances, whether the deceased brought about his death by his own negligence or was killed through the negligence of someone else.

With this majority opinion Justice Black took sharp issue, declaring that an inference might well have been drawn that the deceased did not close the derailer himself since he was an experienced brakeman and well aware of the danger of riding a freight car over a closed derailer. He said:

Twelve North Carolina citizens who heard many witnesses and saw many exhibits found on their oaths that the railroad's employees were negligent. The local trial judge sustained their finding. Four members of this Court agree with the local trial judge that the jury's conclusion was reasonable. Nevertheless five members of the Court purport to weigh all the evidence offered by both parties to the suit, and hold the conclusion was unreasonable. Truly, appellate review of jury verdicts by application of a supposed norm of reasonableness gives rise to puzzling results.[28]

In other personal damage suits Justice Black has followed the same course of reasoning,[29] and has perhaps won the right to be considered the foremost modern champion of trial by jury.

To those who innately resent what seems to them a studied design on the part of courts to exonerate employers for injuries incurred by employees, no judicial doctrine is more odious than that known as "the assumption of risk," which is the rule that in the absence of evidence to the contrary, one who accepts employment impliedly binds himself by contract to assume the dangers commonly incident to it. It is as a corollary to this proposition that the "fellow servant doctrine" derives, for it is upon the reasoning that the negligent habits of a fellow servant is something his co-employees should know about and is a risk which they should be held to assume, that the common law exculpated a master when one of his servants was injured by the negligence of his fellow workman. Thus Edgar Lee Masters lets Butch Weldy tell a typical story:

> After I got religion and steadied down
> They gave me a job in the canning works,
> And every morning I had to fill
> The tank in the yard with gasoline
> That fed the blow fires in the sheds
> To heat the soldering irons.
> And I mounted a rickety ladder to do it,
> Carrying buckets full of the stuff.
> One morning, as I stood there pouring,
> The air grew still and seemed to heave,

120

And I shot up as the tank exploded
And down I came with both legs broken,
And my eyes burned crisp as a couple of eggs.
For someone left a blow fire going,
And something sucked the flame in the tank.
The circuit judge said whoever did it
Was a fellow servant of mine, and so
Old Rhodes' son didn't have to pay me.
And I sat on the witness stand as blind
As Jack the fiddler, saying over and over,
"I didn't know him at all." [30]

Justice Black's opinion in the case of Tiller *v.* Atlantic Coastline Railroad Company [31] reflects a revulsion against the rule almost as pointedly stated as that of the poet. Such a rule, he said, was a judicially created one "to insulate the employer as much as possible from bearing the 'human overhead' which is an inevitable part of the cost—to someone—of doing industrialized business." [32]

Decisions of the Court in which the full faith and credit clause of the Constitution has been used in such a manner as to disadvantage some individual litigant have several times aroused Black to indignant dissent. The case of Magnolia Petroleum Company *v.* Hunt[33] brought about his denunciation of such use of this particular constitutional mandate. The petroleum company had employed Hunt in Louisiana and had sent him to Texas where he sustained an injury compensable under the workmen's compensation law in either state. While still in the hospital in Texas he made application for and was awarded compensation under the Texas statute, and was paid accordingly. When he returned to Louisiana he found that he could have recovered a larger amount under the compensation statute in that state and so brought suit there on which a judgment was rendered for the amount of compensation due under the Louisiana statute less the amount of the payment he had received in Texas. This judgment was reversed by the Supreme Court on the ground that recovery of compensation in one state made the issue *res judicata* in that state and so by virtue of the full faith and credit clause prevented its re-litigation elsewhere.

Viewing the case from a somewhat different angle, Justice Black pointed out that the result of the majority opinion was to give Texas the right to nullify a Louisiana statute. If Louisiana desired to pay a certain amount of compensation to an injured citizen of that state, Black thought that no action of Texas should be permitted to erect a barrier to such payment. "I am not persuaded," he said, "that the full faith and credit clause gives sanction to such control by one state of the internal affairs of another." [34] Then charging that the full faith and credit clause was now being put to the same poor purposes for which the due process clause had so often been employed, he warned his brethren against allowing the Constitution "to become a barrier to free experimentation by the states with the problems of workmen's compensation." [35]

Five years later he had occasion to revert to the same theme.[36] This time a citizen of South Dakota had taken out insurance with an Ohio fraternal benefit society under a contract which required that a claimant seeking to recover death benefits must bring suit within six months from the death of the insured. In South Dakota the applicable statute of limitations allowed six years in which to bring suit. Another South Dakota statute rendered void any stipulation or condition in a contract which limits by agreement the time within which a party may enforce his rights. The question was thus whether the full faith and credit clause required South Dakota to give effect to a provision in the contract of a society incorporated under the laws of Ohio, valid in that state, but ineffective according to the laws of South Dakota.

The five-justice majority, speaking through Justice Burton, held that South Dakota was required to give effect to such a provision of the contract. Had South Dakota objected to the terms of the contract, reasoned the majority, it had been continuously in a position to revoke the society's license to do business in that state or to refuse to renew such license. Since it had done neither, but had allowed the society to operate within its borders, it could not now refuse to give effect to the society's constitution.

Beginning his dissent with a quotation from a century-old opinion of the Court [37] which declared that requiring a state to apply the limitations laws of another state in place of its own would reduce it to vassalage, Justice Black pointed out that what was even worse in the case under consideration was the fact that the state of vassalage to which the Court's decision reduced South Dakota was not even in subordination to the laws of another state, but to a "law" created by a private corporation. Moreover, he was disturbed by the fact that the Court's decision had not limited the principle it laid down to fraternal benefit insurance companies, and foresaw a day when the same legal formula might be applied to protect any corporation doing business in a state other than that in which it was domiciled. The picture he painted was alarming:

123

The result of the Court's opinion, if later carried to its logical conclusion, would be that the policy obligations of all these companies, in whatever state assumed, would be governed by New York or Connecticut law or that of nearby states, and that all of the other states would be deprived of power to pass legislation believed by them to be necessary to protect their own citizens against unconscionable contracts. By permitting its insurance corporations, particularly mutual companies, to make contracts barring an insured's access to state courts, New York, for example, could thus render all the other states helpless to provide a judicial haven for their own wronged citizens. . . .

Hereafter, if today's doctrine should be carried to its logical end, the state in which the most powerful corporations are concentrated, or those corporations themselves, might well be able to pass laws which would govern contracts made by the people in all of the other states.[38]

Yet when Justice Black came to view the North Carolina divorce case [39] that involved the validity of a divorce granted by a Nevada court to a resident of North Carolina, the full faith and credit clause became the cornerstone of his argument. The majority of the Court had sustained a conviction for bigamy of a North Carolinian who had obtained a Nevada divorce, remarried, and returned immediately to North Carolina. It was the contention of the latter state that no *bona fide* domicil had been acquired in Nevada and hence the Nevada court had been without jurisdiction to entertain the divorce suit. The Supreme Court sustained this position but over the strong disapproval of Justice Black who was now shocked at the sight of one state flouting the laws and judicial decrees of another.

Given Justice Black's inclination to look out particularly for the rights of the little man it is not unnatural to expect the obverse side of this disposition to reveal a tendency to suspect bigness solely because of its size. In those cases in which Justice Black has dealt with large corporations wholly apart from their relationship with employees or with small sized competitors, there is some indication of this characteristic. Yet it is well to remember that in almost all these cases the interest of the little man may be affected although his name does not appear as a party upon the legal record. It has already been suggested that Justice Black's voice and vote in behalf of the right of states to tax and control corporate activities within their borders is possibly motivated more by the feeling that there is a necessity for some authority to protect the people, than by a truly jealous apprehension that the incidents of state sovereignty may be narrowed.

It is not difficult to conclude where Justice Black's sympathy would lie in the old-fashioned anti-trust case, although since his appointment to the bench relatively few anti-trust suits have come before the Court. Preparation for war and the necessity for increased production tended to halt such prosecutions, but in those which have reached the Supreme Court Black has shown himself an implacable foe of monopoly and has staunchly supported the government in its effort to control it.[40]

The case of the Associated Press monopoly [41] was well suited to his talents and it was his fortune to be assigned the writing of the Court's opinion. The case brought about a test of the Association's by-laws which conferred upon each member the power to deny membership to any applicant within its district. By this means a competing newspaper could be denied the press service which might be essential to its existence. When Marshall Field's Chicago *Sun* applied for membership it found itself blackballed by the Chicago *Tribune* and thereupon appealed to the Department of

Justice for relief from practices which it charged were in restraint of trade. When the matter reached the Supreme Court Justice Black in a clear, persuasive and well-constructed opinion held the Associated Press guilty of the charge. It was trade restraints of this character, he said, that blocked initiative which brought new-comers into a field of business and thus curtailed the system of free enterprise which the Sherman Act had been intended to pro-tect. To the contention urged by the Association's counsel that the application of the Sherman Act constituted an abridgment of the freedom of the press, Black had a ready answer:

It would be strange indeed . . . if the grave concern for the freedom of the press which prompted adoption of the First Amendment should be read as a command that the government was without power to protect that freedom. The First Amendment, far from providing an argument against application of the Sherman Act, here provides powerful reasons to the contrary. That Amendment rests on the assumption that the widest pos-sible dissemination of information from diverse and antagonistic sources is essential to the welfare of the public, that a free press is a condition of a free society. Surely a command that the government itself shall not im-pede the free flow of ideas does not afford non-governmental combinations a refuge if they impose restraints upon that constitutionally guaranteed freedom. Freedom to publish means freedom for all and not for some. Freedom to publish is guaranteed by the Constitution, but freedom to combine to keep others from publishing is not.[42]

It is impossible to consider this decision without remembering that Justice Black suffered much at the hands of the press and without speculating upon the personal satisfaction that he may have derived from writing an opinion which stripped from the smug and powerful organization of newspapers its claim of a right to engage in monopolistic practices upon the pretense that it was merely a voluntary organization for cooperation among members and so entitled to restrict membership as it saw fit.

Still another indication of Justice Black's conviction that the public interest ofter suffers through the machinations of concentrated commercial and industrial power is shown by his opinions in patent cases. The misuse of the privilege attending patent rights has been notorious and the application of the law creating the exclusive right to use new inventions has sometimes served to discourage rather than promote invention.[43] Cases are numerous where patent rights have been bought not for the purpose of manufacturing products thereunder, but to stifle competition. Justice Black has made it plain that he understands how the purpose of the patent law may be perverted.

Early in his judicial career he took exception to a majority opinion written in a patent case [44] by no less an opponent of monopoly than Justice Brandeis. A patent pool which controlled the manufacture of sound amplifiers had granted exclusive licenses to the Western Electric Company for production for the commercial field. Other manufacturers were licensed by the pool to make amplifiers for private or home use. One of this latter group of licensees manufactured amplifiers which were suitable for theaters. In the suit instituted by Western Electric Company Justice Brandeis said that the practice of granting licenses for restricted use was an old one whose "legality has never been questioned." [45]

Its legality was to be questioned in short order, however, for Justice Black in a dissenting opinion declared that when an article described in a patent was sold and passed into the hands of the purchaser it was "no longer within the limits of the monopoly." [46]. To allow the holder of a patent to attach such strings to the sale of a patented article so as to control use after sale, Black thought was an evil which the patent law had not been invented to accomplish.

Moreover, he would have a strict policy pursued in granting patents and is convinced that they have often been granted improvidently upon unpatentable material. In one instance he dissented from an opinion of the Court which held that a machine involving only the use of old mechanical constructions was patentable when it combined them in such a way as to produce an improved result. In his attack upon this position he said:

One who invents improvements on a prior invention, whether his own or someone else's, may patent the improvements separately. But I do not believe that our patent system was intended to allow the indiscriminate jumbling of the new and old which would permit the inventor of improvements to extend his domain of monopoly by perpetuating rights in old inventions beyond the seventeen year period Congress has provided.[47]

Charging that the patented device now in question was "an attempt to utilize minor improvements to perpetuate exclusive enjoyment of a major instrument of production which rightfully belongs to the public," he pointed out that such patents had an "interminable capacity for self-perpetuation." [48]

Moreover, Black is unwilling to agree that the question of patentability involves merely a finding of fact. In the case of Graver Tank and Manufacturing Co. *v.* Linde Air Products Co.[49] he dissented from the opinion of the Court which declared that the Supreme Court should not undertake to review the concurrent findings of the two lower courts concerning the patentability of an item. As he views the matter, such a question is one of law upon which the Supreme Court may properly review decisions of lower courts.

Still another quarrel that Justice Black has with the interpretation of the patent law is that the failure of a patentee to make use of the patented invention is held not to affect the validity of the patent. In an instance where such a rule was reaffirmed by a majority of the Court he joined with Justice Douglas in criticizing it as a brake upon the progress of technology. "How," asked the dissenters, "may the words, 'to make, use, and vend,' be read to mean, 'not to make, not to use, and not to vend?' " [50]

An examination of Justice Black's opinions and votes in the foregoing cases reveals no attachment to any single constitutional principle so deep that all other considerations are subordinate. For example, although he frequently professes respect for the reservations guaranteed to the states by the Tenth Amendment, when a state by an anti-trust law undertook to restrict the operation of union picket lines, he was quick to declare that it had overstepped its authority. Similarly, although he upheld as a personal right the power of a group of workers to reject for any reason the application of would-be members, such a personal right to select associates paled noticeably when relied on to justify a monopoly in the dissemination of news.

Just as he seems little interested in the question of federalism, *per se,* so he is rather indifferent to the naked constitutional principles stemming from the contract clause or the full faith and credit provision. He appears to look upon them quite candidly as tools with which to attain an end, and as such he employs them in his effort to help the poor and weak in their struggle against the more powerful.

CHAPTER VIII

EQUAL AND EXACT JUSTICE

When it is said that Justice Black has been consistently watchful to protect the interests of "the little man" something should be added lest the term be too narrowly construed. It is not confined to the poor nor to those oppressed by the operation of major social and political forces, but stretches far enough to include all who for any reason are hard put to maintain their rights in an unequal conflict. In this category fall often the enemies of society caught and held helpless by the machinery of avenging justice. Most law-abiding citizens give little heed when these offenders complain against the method by which law is administered, and the procedural provisions to which they sometimes appeal are commonly despised as "legal technicalities."

In extenuation of the public attitude it should be said that it arises largely from an ignorance of what goes on behind the curtain of law enforcement. It is assumed that the rack and wheel have no counterparts in means today employed to detect crime and milder methods are commonly condoned as necessary to a worthy end. Thus in a widely circulated magazine a former chief of the United States Secret Service has told how evidence was obtained of an income tax evasion by putting one of the suspect's accomplices in a "special" cell—special in that it had been filled with vermin—where the bites of bed-bugs in due time brought out incriminating testimony.[1] So far as known the story shocked no part

130

of the public conscience for the man convicted by the evidence so obtained was so notorious for misdeeds that his character appeared to justify whatever means were employed to destroy him.

Justice Black regards such reasoning as vicious error. That the little man may be a bad man, does not, in his opinion, denude him of human and constitutional rights, nor warrant a court in watering them down until they are no more than colorable. Clearly he is an advocate of the English accusatorial system of prosecuting crime as contrasted with the inquisitiorial method pursued on the continent, and does not equivocate between the two because the latter sometimes excels in the efficiency with which it detects and punishes. It is the accusing sovereign's business in criminal actions, he thinks, to make out its case like any other plaintiff in strict observance of the constitutional rights of the defendant. From this determination to protect the rights of a criminal caught in the toils of the law have come some of his best reasoned and most convincing opinions. His utterance in one such case moved Charles A. Beard to declare that it should be read by all citizens "who care for the perpetuity of the Republic," and to predict that it would "ring with power as long as liberty and justice are cherished." [2]

This was in the case of Chambers v. Florida[3] where Justice Black, speaking eloquently for the Court, reversed the judgment of the Supreme Court of Florida which had affirmed the death sentence of four Negro men. The record in the case left it uncertain whether actual physical violence had been applied in order to obtain the confession upon which the men had been convicted, but it was shown that for a full week after their arrests they were continually quizzed without being able to obtain counsel or see friends. For five days no confession was forthcoming, but finally after a period of questioning that lasted from three o'clock one afternoon until the next morning, their resistence broke. Commenting upon the situation Justice Black said:

The record . . . shows, without conflict, the drag net methods of arrest on suspicion without warrant, and the protracted questioning and cross questioning of these ignorant young colored tenant farmers by State officers and other white citizens, in a fourth floor jail room, where as prisoners they were without friends, advisers or counselors, and under circumstances calculated to break the strongest nerves and the stoutest resistance. . . .

The very circumstances surrounding their confinement and their questioning without any formal charges having been brought, were such as to fill petitioners with terror and frightful misgivings. . . . The haunting fear of mob violence was around them in an atmosphere charged with excitement and public indignation. . . .

To permit human lives to be forfeited upon confessions thus obtained would make of the constitutional requirement of due process of law a meaningless symbol. . . . No higher duty, no more solemn responsibility, rests upon this Court, than that of translating into living law and maintaining this constitutional shield deliberately planned and inscribed for the benefit of every human being subject to our Constitution—of whatever race, creed or persuasion.[4]

The *Catholic World* which had called Justice Black's appointment "a first class calamity," now praised him for this decision and quoted with approval a newspaper which had referred to it as "far and away the most direct, sweeping, and brilliantly written application of the Fourteenth Amendment to human rights that has come from our highest court." [5]

Similar sentiments have been voiced by Justice Black upon other occasions. In California a veritable Bluebeard was convicted of the murder of his wife. In relays state officers questioned the accused from seven one Sunday evening until the next morning when he was allowed to eat breakfast, after which the interrogations were resumed and continued until three o'clock Tuesday morning, at which time, according to the statement of the officers, he "fell asleep." At any rate, he was no longer conscious and the inquisitors temporarily desisted from their efforts to obtain incriminating admissions. In a subsequent effort, however, they were successful. A majority of the Court was unwilling to interfere with the judgment of conviction and thought the irregularities complained of were not important enough to infect fatally the trial with that absence of fairness necessary to constitute a denial of due process.[6]

Justice Black balked at this conclusion. He did not have to be told how easy it was for those who deal with the detection and punishment of crime to graduate from zeal to brutality. He considered that the coercion of the accused was sufficiently shown to warrant reversal, and declared that the third degree should end somewhere short of the point where the person questioned lost consciousness.

In another case where this sort of police pressure had been resorted to[7] Justice Black spoke for the Court's majority. A man suspected of murder had been arrested in Memphis where the administration of criminal law has long been notorious and where the police, without benefit of civil service, answer directly to a political boss. Naturally in this environment police methods continue to be among the country's crudest. Here they had interrogated the arrested man continuously from seven o'clock one Saturday evening until next Monday morning at half past nine, during which time, while the officers questioned him in relays, he

133

had not been allowed to leave the room until he finally made the statement they desired. Of this procedure Justice Black wrote:

We think a situation such as that here shown by uncontradicted evidence is so inherently coercive that its very existence is irreconcilable with the possession of mental freedom by a lone suspect against whom its full coercive force is brought to bear. It is inconceivable that any court of justice in the land, conducted as our courts are, open to the public, would permit prosecutors serving in relays to keep a defendant witness under continuous cross examination for thirty-six hours without rest or sleep in an effort to extract a "voluntary" confession. Nor can we, consistently with Constitutional due process of law, hold voluntary a confession where prosecutors do the same thing away from the restraining influences of a public trial in an open court room.[8]

Justice Jackson, with whom Justices Roberts and Frankfurter concurred, dissented. He objected that the Court's opinion had fixed a particular period of time as too long to keep a suspect under examination instead of making the question a more abstract one of whether the suspect was in full possession of his will and self-control at the time of the confession. Some men, he said, can stand a much longer period of interrogation than others, so that the test should not be how long the treatment continued but what had been the effect of it. Also in this dissent Justice Jackson expressed the typical philosophy of those who defend the use of torture to produce evidence: the burden of protecting society, he said, is on the state, and the courts should not take from it what legal means it has to perform this task. The weasel word is readily discovered in the term "legal." The Justice who had got acquainted with police methods as a city judge in Birmingham thought that the application of the third degree for more than thirty-eight hours was not legal, while the Justice who had done his private law practice in the quiet little town of Jamestown, New York, and knew police methods chiefly from written records, was able to take a more tolerant view.

Another principle that Justice Black has ardently espoused is the right of every man, guilty or innocent, to be advised and represented by counsel. In Adams *v.* United States[9] the record showed that in a criminal case tried in a United States district court a defendant had deliberately elected not to be represented and had waived trial by jury. The majority of the Court, in an opinion by Justice Frankfurter, sustained the conviction upon the ground of waiver, but Justices Black, Douglas and Murphy thought that the waiver of jury trial was such an important matter that it ought not to be permitted without the advice of competent counsel. Logically, the effect of this view would seem to force counsel upon a man who did not wish it, but this objection fell before the fact of the disadvantage under which they knew a defendant without a lawyer labored. Again in the case of a German spy who had waived her right to counsel Black voted to reverse the conviction on the ground that she had not had "that full understanding and comprehension of her legal rights indispensable to a valid waiver of assistance of counsel." [10] He criticized the trial judge for merely asking the accused whether she desired counsel and declared that by such a routine inquiry the judge had not informed himself "of the facts essential to an informed decision that an accused has executed a valid waiver of his right to counsel." [11]

It was in connection with the right to counsel that Justice Black first began his campaign to persuade the Court that the prohibitions and guaranties of the Bill of Rights applied to the states as well as to the national government. This position was confronted by substantial precedent, for the Court had repeatedly held that the first eight amendments applied exclusively to a citizen's relations with the federal government. The history of the amendments indicated that purpose on the part of those who framed them and until the adoption of the Fourteenth Amendment there had been no doubt that the Bill of Rights limited federal power only. Chief Justice Marshall had observed that the question was one "of great importance, but not much difficulty." [12] After the enactment of the Fourteenth Amendment the question had been raised whether the new amendment applied to the states the provisions by which the older amendments had limited the powers of the federal government. This question the Court had repeatedly answered in the negative,[13] but Justice Black now stated, "I believe that the Fourteenth Amendment made the Sixth applicable to the States." [14]

In the case that called forth this startling declaration a Maryland state court had refused to appoint counsel for an indigent defendant who requested it, telling him that the rule of the court in the county wherein he was being tried was that counsel would be appointed only in cases involving a charge of murder or rape. The Supreme Court, in an opinion by Justice Roberts, restated the long-accepted view that the Sixth Amendment applied only to trials in federal courts. This left the determinative question that of whether the refusal to furnish counsel to a defendant requesting it constituted a denial of due process. This was answered in the negative and the conviction was sustained.

Justice Black began his dissent by painting a picture of the defendant, a farm hand, out of work and on relief, uneducated and without friends or advisers. He then stated his proposition that the Fourteenth Amendment operated to make the Sixth applicable to the states. But even if this were not so, he said, the case should still be reversed upon the ground that a fair trial, one of the elements of due process, had not been accorded the defendant. Denial to the poor of the request for counsel, he said, "has long been regarded as shocking to the 'universal sense of justice' throughout this country." [15]

There have been cases, however, in which Black decided that defendants had been duly represented notwithstanding their claim to the contrary. In one case where it was urged that counsel had not had sufficient time to prepare the defendant's case Black spoke for the Court and dismissed the contention as unsubstantial.[16] He found that the trial court on Monday had appointed two attorneys to defend the accused, and that it was on the following Thursday that their motion for a continuance had been denied. Pointing out that the case, which had arisen in his native state, had been tried in a rural county whose county seat had a population of less than a thousand and where it was relatively easy to obtain information concerning both events and witnesses, he expressed the opinion that the time permitted for the preparation of the case had been entirely adequate. What more they could have done had additional time been allowed, counsel had failed to state.

In the case of Canizio v. New York,[17] Justice Black again exhibited his practical side and showed that he was not altogether governed by his emotions in cases of this nature. Here a plea of guilty had been entered without benefit of counsel and, although adequate representation had been obtained subsequent to this plea, the accused argued that he had been denied the right to counsel since he had not had it at every step of the proceedings. Justice Black did not agree. His lawyer, he said, could have withdrawn the plea of guilty if he had thought it advisable. The fact that he did not indicated that he considered it to the best interest of his client to allow the plea to stand. Justices Murphy and Rutledge, who had had less experience in rough and tumble trial practice than Justice Black, dissented, insisting that "the right to counsel means nothing unless it means the right to counsel at each and every step in a criminal proceeding." [18]

In only five instances has Justice Black voted to declare acts of Congress unconstitutional and one of these votes was against a statute that seemed to him to sap the substance of jury trial.[19] The Federal Firearms Act had provided that it should be unlawful for any person who had been convicted of a crime of violence to receive any firearms or ammunition that had been shipped in interstate commerce. Moreover it had declared that the possession of firearms or ammunition by any such person should constitute presumptive evidence that the same had been shipped or transported in interstate commerce in violation of the law, a provision obviously intended to shift the burden of proof to the defendant.

In spite of his disinclination to strike down acts of Congress, Black could not approve this one which authorized juries to convict defendants even in cases where the government offered no evidence tending to prove "an essential ingredient of the offense." He believed that any verdict against a defendant had to be preceded by the introduction of some evidence logically tending to prove the elements of the crime charged and that a statute which raised a presumption of guilt without such evidence violated the due process clause of the Fifth Amendment.

Another method of circumscribing the full benefit of jury trial that fell under Justice Black's condemnation is the practice of impaneling special or "blue ribbon" juries to serve in certain types of cases. A New York statute had prescribed standards for the selection of the "blue ribbon jurors,"[20] and whether or not veniremen met such standards was not determined by the court in the customary manner but through the procedure of having each prospective juror testify before the county clerk. The majority of the Supreme Court could see nothing unconstitutional in such a system, but to Justice Black it appeared another step toward the destruction of trial by jury. He joined in a dissent written by Justice Murphy which declared that such selection of a jury tended to obliterate its representative character and denied to a litigant tried before it "his Constitutional right to be tried by a jury fairly drawn from a cross section of the community."[21] A man who was qualified to serve on the general jury panel, the dissenters thought, should be qualified to serve upon any jury, and they made plain their suspicion of hand-picked juries drawn from the so-called "better element" of the community.

Necessity for the complete impartiality of jurors has also been strongly stated by Justice Black. After Eugene Dennis, the Secretary General of the Communist Party in the United States, had been tried and convicted in the District of Columbia for contempt of the House Committee on Un-American Activities he sought a reversal of the conviction pleading that he had not been accorded an impartial jury as guaranteed by the Sixth Amendment. Seven of the twelve jurors who convicted him were government employees and it was his contention that such jurors, aware of the current loyalty check of government employees, would fear to vote for his acquittal lest such a course be interpreted as " sympathetic association " with communism. This contention the majority of the Court dismissed. There was no substantial indication, they thought, that government employees were so intimidated by the threat of investigation that they were unable to perform their duty as jurors.[22]

Justice Black in dissent declared that it was "wholly unrealistic" to expect such employees "to enter the jury box with that quality of disinterestedness essential to complete impartiality" in view of the "prevailing pattern of loyalty investigations and threatened purges." [23] In his opinion government employees had good reason to fear that a vote for the acquittal of an avowed Communist might bring about their discharge or an embarrasing investigation and consequently to expect from them complete impartiality was "to disregard human nature."

Likewise Justice Black has severely denounced juries, both grand and petit, from which members of minority groups have been systematically excluded and has refused to be satisfied by a mere token compliance with the rule which forbids their exclusion. In one case that came before the Court from Texas the jury commission had selected a panel containing the name of one Negro, a concessive procedure designed to satisfy the letter of the law.[24] The majority of the Court thought such compliance sufficient to meet the demands of the Constitution, but not so Justice Black. He and Chief Justice Stone were unable to agree that the commission's act in placing the name of a single Negro on the panel was a substantial compliance which satisfied the requirement of due process. Once again Black was voting to consider substance rather than form.[25]

One of the best examples of Justice Black's insistence upon a fair trial is furnished by the case involving the military courts in Hawaii.[26] Immediately after the attack on Pearl Harbor the Governor of Hawaii issued a proclamation placing the territory under martial law. Both criminal and civil courts were closed and superseded by military tribunals, the judgments of which were not subject to direct appellate review. Two years later and after the regular courts had resumed their normal functions these military agencies were still insisting upon trying all criminal cases that resulted from alleged violations of military orders. Since such orders were unrestricted in scope they soon involved many sorts of day-by-day conduct entirely unrelated, except by the broadest stretch of imagination, to the welfare of the armed forces or the efficiency of their operations. One civilian who defrauded another was said thereby to violate military rule and so to be subject to punishment by the military tribunal. Laborers absent from their jobs were promptly jailed under the application of wartime regulations which had frozen them to their employment, a procedure not altogether objectionable to their employers.

As is usual under military government the ordinary processes of law were despised as dilatory and inconvenient, and the procedure conventionally required for the protection of civil rights was suspended upon the theory of *inter arma leges silent.* These tribunals did not actually follow Falstaff's advice as to the method of getting rid of lawyers, but merely let it be known that such adjuncts of judicial practice were quite a handicap to a defendant. To many who knew that they were going to be convicted anyhow it seemed best not to incur the displeasure of military officers by attempting a defense. In short, these trials went far to justify the definition of a court martial as a judicial agency to convict defendants, and even in Hawaii, long accustomed to military dominance, such proceedings became a stench in the nostrils of residents who retained any respect for civil liberty. Most of the evils which commonly attend an army's assumption of civil functions disgraced the military administration of justice.[27] Finally two civilians, sentenced by a military court for offenses wholly unconnected with army occupation, challenged the court's jurisdiction to try them and ultimately carried their cases before the Supreme Court.

A case better built to provoke the feelings of Justice Black can hardly be imagined nor one more worthy of his talent for scorching criticism. Here rolled into one case were the several trial procedures he had singly denounced as denials of due process. Lack of counsel, absence of trial by jury, suspension of the writ of *habeas corpus,* and a pervading element of coercion were all present. The Little Tailor who killed seven at a blow had no more inviting target.

Many wondered whether the rule announced by the Supreme Court in 1866 in the case *Ex Parte Milligan*[28] would be adhered to. That rule is that so long as civil courts are open and able to function citizens shall not be tried by the military for civil offenses.

"Martial law," Justice Davis had said, "cannot arise from a threatened invasion. The necessity must be actual and present, the invasion real, and such as effectively closes the courts and deposes civil administration." [29] But this test, said critics, had evolved when armies travelled on foot and was an anachronism in this day when troops are air-borne.

Justice Black, writing for the majority of the Court, declined to take any stock in such a contention. He thought the doctrine of the Milligan case sound and applicable. Noting that at the time the two defendants were tried business was being carried on as usual, public buildings were open, and civil courts functioning, he reaffirmed the Milligan rule and said:

Courts and their procedural safeguards are indispensable to our system of government. They were set up by the founders to protect the liberties they valued. Our system of government clearly is the antithesis of total military rule and the founders of this country are not likely to have contemplated complete military dominance within the limits of a Territory made part of this country.[30]

In a dissenting opinion delivered in the case of Johnson v. Eisentrager[31] Justice Black argued that in a *habeas corpus* proceeding neither the location of the petitioner nor his status as an enemy alien ought in times of peace prevent his resort to the constitutional writ so long as he was being held prisoner under United States authority. The petitioners were German nationals convicted by a military commission of continuing hostilities against the United States subsequent to the German surrender by cooperating with the still belligerent Japanese. They were later repatriated and filed their suit while being held prisoners in Germany. Justice

143

Jackson, speaking for the Court's majority, said that no case had been found in the history of any nation where the writ of *habeas corpus* is recognized, allowing its employment by an enemy alien not within the Court's geographical jurisdiction. Such an innovation, he thought, unwarranted and inexpedient.

Justice Black, with whom Justices Douglas and Burton concurred, refused to be governed by the want of precedent or the apprehension of inconvenient consequences that might flow from a broadened jurisdiction. He thought that jurisdiction to entertain a petition for the writ properly existed in the Federal courts in any case where a petitioner was being held prisoner under the authority of the United States Government. " Conquest by the United States," he said, " does not mean tyranny," [32] and insisted that his country's warranty of justice ought to be co-extensive with its authority and that the ancient legal device invented to implement this warranty ought to be available wherever the flag flew.

Justice Black's insistence upon the observance of both the letter and the spirit of the constitutional guaranties of fair trial stands as one of his major contributions to judicial literature. More experienced than his colleagues in the realities of criminal practice, he is probably more keenly aware of the methods by which the springs of justice are sometimes dammed or polluted. He realizes that man's inhumanity to man may be found in a court house as well as elsewhere and that the poor, weak, friendless, and ignorant are often incidentally crushed by the mechanics of a system built for a better purpose. His yet unsuccessful campaign to apply to the states all the restrictions of the first eight amendments is no doubt strengthened if not inspired by his persuasion that the state courts as well as the federal have need to be held to a humane administration of penal law by written rules embodied in a national bill of rights.

Yet this attitude is begot of no morbid compassion for the criminal nor any predisposition toward leniency for those accused of crime. He is not led by sympathy to temper with tears a righteous judgment against one fairly condemned. His determination to see that a fair trial is accorded the unworthy as well as the worthy does not lead him into captious criticism of every procedural irregularity nor prevent his being able to look through the veil of specious argument so often made by convicted defendants. He is as willing as any of his colleagues to sweep aside assignments of error where he is able to see that the defendant had a fair trial notwithstanding, but he is not willing to do so merely because of the culprit's depravity or the apparent probability of his guilt. He knows that unless a rule is strong enough to be invoked by the guilty it can be of little use to the innocent and therefore scrupulously opposes a tendency to condone departure from constitutional guaranties on the mere ground that some recognized malefactor may profit by their application. In no other class of cases has he shown a stronger devotion to the elementary principles of fair play and unsullied justice.

CHAPTER IX

THE RIGHTS OF MAN AND OF THE CITIZEN

Closely akin to the guaranty of fair trial are those provisions of the first eight amendments framed to secure certain personal liberties which the people of the United States claim as rights and with which, as they have been taught, the founders of their nation meant to brook no interference. Thus the freedom of thought, expression, assembly and petition, protected by the First Amendment, has come to be accepted by Americans as an essential cornerstone of self-government, and it is our custom to appraise the political progress of other states by the degree in which such freedom is tolerated or prohibited. Not only do we regard these restraints upon government as proper, but as limitations so fundamental to the existence of democracy as to become a part of its very definition. If the term "democracy" means no more than the general direction of governmental policy by the majority of the people it is, in the opinion of most Americans, not worth the effort that has been spent in its evolution and they would warn any people bent on adopting such a government that they may be but swapping the devil for the witch. There are some kinds of authority which we are no more willing to confer upon a majority of our fellow citizens than upon a selected few. To the man tyrannically despoiled there is no balm in being told that his spoliation was determined upon by a plebiscite. Neither will the man who has glimpsed a new planet or found a neoteric road to heaven willingly submit his discovery to "the common sense of most" and abide by the quantitative judgment of his peers as to whether he shall cherish or discard it.

Whatever it meant in Athens, the word "democracy" today denotes something more than majority rule. Indeed one eminent authority has said, "a democratic state is always a limited state." [1] Whether the limitations be written or traditional may be but a matter of method, but when a governing body is entirely without restraints it is properly regarded as a tyranny, altogether apart from the question of whether or not it acts with wide popular support. The voice of the people is the voice of God only in the sense that it is irresistible. In point of probity its orders may be as devilish as those of Nero. With this realization wise men have devised what they call "constitutional limitations" and various sorts of personal liberty flourish only because of such protection.

To be sure not all of the same freedoms are to be found in every democracy. Soil and climate encourage many variations and each seems to grow best in the region to which it is native. Yet to conceive of a democracy without any of them is to envision a political desert made habitable by no shelter from the caprice of winds or the severity of weather.

Also it is to be remembered that these limitations on government were generated as political principles under widely differing circumstances and still bear birthmarks indicating their origin. Religious freedom, for example, was hardly a philosophic principle with the populace for whom our founding fathers spoke. Many of their ancestors had come to America for freedom to worship God in a particular way and to compel everyone else to do likewise. Stern theocracy still cast its shadow across the colonies

147

and the agreement upon religious freedom was perhaps nothing more than an accommodation of views under the only canopy broad enough to cover them. The diversity of doctrine among the communities and the utter impossibility of a consensus upon any particular religious form left no path to be followed except that pointed out by a few men who were actual advocates of religious liberty and believed in freedom of worship as a matter of principle. These men made headway because joint action and eventual union could not be accomplished except by fastening upon the national government a purely negative policy. Therefore "Congress shall make no law respecting the establishment of religion."

The freedom of expression, assembly and petition, on the other hand, had its roots in deeper attachment to theoretical principle forged and tempered in the fire of English experience. Yet it cannot be said that these older landmarks of liberty are now more a matter of principle with Americans than is the newer doctrine of religious freedom. So it is through the whole list of liberties we are taught to cherish. Often they developed separately but always in the end each reinforced the others. For instance in many cases determined by the Supreme Court it is impossible to say whether the decision turned mainly on religious liberty or the freedom of speech.

Naturally enough, neither nations nor men set the same store upon the several limitations which democracy requires, although a single sentence in the First Amendment was broad enough to comprehend the most fundamenal. Seldom does an individual display the same degree of attachment to each separate principle of personal liberty, and here as elsewhere emotional choices often

148

baffle analysis. Yet a judge's understanding of values and the general direction of his strongest hopes and fears are often indicated by the consistency and tenacity with which he holds to certain principles of liberty while conceding something to the exigencies of practical application in the case of others.

Since few in this day ever assert that any sort of personal liberty is entirely without qualification, the qualifications themselves become rather heterogeneous in composition and mental attitudes may be reflected by the degree of hospitality with which the several kinds of qualifications are entertained. For example, we are all agreed that no one may defame, trespass, or annoy with impunity by claiming the protection of the broad language of the Bill of Rights. As blackguards are answerable for slanderous words and as the right of assembly furnishes no mitigation for trespass upon private property, so all such rights are somewhat limited by other legal and conventional concepts. Now and then courts are called upon to say whether some modification of the absolute goes far enough to constitute an infringement and herein lies the field for difference which so often becomes the battleground for conflicting theories.

Undoubtedly the course of construction has been to broaden and dignify certain prohibitions of the Bill of Rights beyond their express words. Particularly has this been true in the case of the First Amendment whose terms, although relating expressly to the powers of congress, have been construed to flow through the Fourteenth Amendment to become effective also against the states. The present Supreme Court has been distinguished by its championship of civil liberties, even to a point which has caused some

149

competent observers to view its liberality with alarm.[2] It is here intended to note instances in which Justice Black has stood in the forefront of the Court's progress in this direction along with those wherein he has seemed to lag behind some of his brethren in his willingness to pursue principle against the argument of national necessity or the promotion of common welfare. No member of the Court has been more determined than Justice Black to protect the freedom of conscience and of expression. In an early opinion he made clear his devotion to the prohibitions of the First Amendment when he said:

I view the guaranties of the First Amendment as the foundation upon which our governmental structure rests and without which it could not continue to endure as conceived and planned. Freedom to speak and write about public questions is as important as is the heart to the human body. In fact, this privilege is the heart of our government. If that heart be weakened, the result is debilitation; if it be stilled, the result is death.[3]

To this creed he has steadily adhered.

To certain other constitutional limitations Justice Black has shown somewhat less devotion. For example, he has been willing to sanction searches and seizures which seemed unreasonable to other members of the Court, and he voted to hold constitutional a wartime statute which operated to remove thousands of Americans of Japanese extraction from their homes on the West coast without any pretense that they had been guilty of any offense. Likewise he has shown less disposition than some of his brethren to allow those accused of treason to invoke successfully the protection of constitutional provisions. As much as he is attached to these tenets of freedom, he can conceive that strict adherence to a course they would compel in times of peace may endanger the country's very existence in time of war. He seems to agree with the reasoning expressed by President Lincoln when he suspended the writ of *habeas corpus,* that if a limb need be sacrificed to save the body the limb must go.

Cases involving religious freedom fall readily into two categories, those in which the state is charged with restricting some religious practice, and antithetically, those in which it is charged with preference or subsidy. In the first group Justice Black has been usually in favor of the complaining litigant who desired to pursue some religious course without secular interference. In the second group his course has not been so consistent.

Most of the cases involving the freedom of religion that have reached the Court since Justice Black's appointment have been occasioned by the activities of a persistent group of fanatics known as Jehovah's Witnesses, which has successfully utilized the courts of the land to argue its cause and attract the attention of the nation. Rarely does a term of the Supreme Court end without at least one decision concerning this sect which it seems might well have chosen the appellation "Jehovah's Litigants." Justice Black's record of consistency in upholding the claims of this "peculiar people" is extremely high.

In the case of Jones *v.* Opelika[4] the constitutionality of a license fee was involved. The fee in question was a privilege tax upon the sale of all magizines and pamphlets with no mark of discrimination either against or in favor of those relating to religion. It is difficult to conceive a situation under which such a law applicable not only to all sales of the publications of the

151

divers religious sects but likewise to the sale of all secular publications, could ever be made the means of oppression or suppression, and Justice Reed writing the opinion of the Court, held that when religious groups use ordinary avenues of commerce they may properly be required to pay the toll exacted of other travellers on the same highway. Here a religious group was employing ordinary commercial methods, selling tracts for the purpose of raising funds. The Court therefore held that the state was free to impose upon such activity the same reasonable fees for the privilege of canvassing to which such activity was subject when pursued by secular agencies. Justice Black however, considered the license tax, as applied to religious groups, an unconstitutional restriction upon religious freedom and hence dissented from the opinion of the Court. One year later the Court accepted the position of the dissenters and formally reversed its earlier opinion.[5]

The spoken word was to come in for its triumphant day in court in the case of Martin *v.* Struthers[6] where there was drawn in question a municipal ordinance which forbade peddlers, solicitors, or advertisers of any sort to go from house to house, knocking on doors or ringing bells. It was urged that the city of Struthers had very good reason for such an ordinance since it was an industrial community where a large part of the inhabitants worked at night and slept during the day, and to whom door knockers and bell pushers were a nuisance. Jehovah's Witnesses, contentious as ever, challenged the ordinance as interference with their religious activities. Their Bible had commanded them to "go into all the world and preach the gospel to every creature," and they thought

152

they were but pursuing this divine injunction when they went from house to house carrying phonographs to which they asked residents to listen and handing out leaflets which they requested them to read. To Justice Black the right of a night worker to sleep during the day without being pestered seemed not so important as the protection of religious freedom. Since the Witnesses saw fit to employ door to door visits to proselyte for their faith, he considered their visits a religious practice and held the city's interference an infringement upon religious freedom. Here again, it may be observed, the shadow of the little man fell across his reasoning. " Door to door distribution of circulars," he said, " is essential to the poorly financed causes of little people." [7] Moreover, he considered freedom to distribute information "so clearly vital to the preservation of a free society that, putting aside reasonable police and health regulations . . . it must be freely preserved." [8]

Justices Reed, Roberts, and Jackson thought that the ordinance was a "reasonable police regulation" which did not objectionably restrict the freedom of speech or the freedom of religion. But it had begun to appear that the majority of the Court was willing to go a long way toward an agreement with Justice Black's distrust of the assertion of any sovereign power that might even incidentally limit the individual's right to worship, speak, or print according to the dictates of his conscience.[9]

It remained for the case of Marsh v. Alabama[10] to call forth Justice Black's most vigorous assertion of the right of minority religious groups to conduct their proselyting campaigns, free not only from the restrictions of legislation, but also from the common-law rules relating to the rights of ownership. Here the town of Chickasaw, Alabama, was established upon land owned by the Gulf Shipbuilding Corporation, and signs were posted around the town reading: "This is private property, and without written permission no street, or house vendor, agent or solicitor of any kind will be permitted." A member of the Jehovah's Witnesses, disdaining such warning, stationed herself upon a street and began handing out pamphlets. When she succeeded in getting herself arrested for trespassing she insisted that the corporation's rule could not be constitutionally applied to her, since so to apply it would violate her freedom of religion. Justice Black agreed with her and said:

Ownership does not always mean absolute dominion. The more an owner, for his advantage, opens up his property for use by the public in general, the more do his rights become circumscribed by the statutory and constitutional rights of those who use it. . . .

Whether a corporation or a municipality owns or possesses the town the public in either case has an identical interest in the functioning of the community in such a manner that the channels of communication remain free. . . . The managers appointed by the corporation cannot curtail the liberty of press and religion of these people consistently with the purposes of the Constitutional guarantees, and a state statute which enforces such action . . . clearly violates the First and Fourteenth Amendments to the Constitution. . . .

When we balance the constitutional rights of owners of property against those of the people to enjoy freedom of press and religion, as we must here, we remain mindful of the fact that the latter occupy a preferred position.[11]

In one instance, however, Justice Black's practicality would not allow him to go so far as one of his colleagues in unfettering from the state's police power the right to propagandize in behalf of faith. In the case of Prince *v.* Massachusetts[12] this freedom came in

154

conflict with a Massachusetts child labor law which forbade children to sell papers or magazines in the public streets. Such a prohibition, said a member of the Jehovah's Witnesses, denied both to her and to her nine-year-old daughter their religious liberty. The child herself was said to be an ordained minister of the faith who was properly practicing her evangelical mission by offering to sell religious tracts in the streets and hence was outside the scope of the statute. This reasoning was going a little too far for Justice Black who now deserted the Witnesses and agreed with the Court's majority that society's power to regulate child labor could not be nullified by so flimsy an argument. Justice Murphy alone took the contrary view, declaring that the freedom of worship was paramount and that wherever such freedom was even incidentally interfered with the burden was upon the state to justify such incidental interference by proving its necessity. In the case at bar such necessity, he thought, had not been proved.

The second class of suits involving the issue of religious freedom is exemplified by the case of Everson v. Board of Education[13] where the question of religious freedom had arisen, not because a state or its instrumentality was attempting to deprive someone of such asserted freedom, but because the state of New Jersey was moving in a manner that seemed to favor a religious organization. The state had authorized its local school districts to contract for the transportation of children to and from schools, and one township, rather than provide special school buses, reimbursed parents for their expense in sending their children to public and parochial schools on the regular commercial buses. Because part of the money so refunded was sent to parents whose children attended Catholic schools a disgruntled taxpayer protested that this was an example of a state paying out public money to support an instrument of a particular church and so violative of the Fourteenth Amendment.[14]

Justice Black, writing the opinion of the Court, answered that the same amendment that prevents New Jersey from establishing a religion, likewise commands the state not to hamper its citizens in the free exercise of religion. Thus, he continued, the state cannot exclude members of any religion from the benefits of public welfare legislation. Police detailed to regulate the traffic in school zones are not prohibited from directing traffic in front of Catholic institutions, he pointed out, and the duty of firemen requires them to work just as hard to put out a fire in a parochial school as in a public school. The Fourteenth Amendment, he said, does not require the state to be the adversary of any religion and "state power is no more to be used so as to handicap religions than it is to favor them." [15]

Four Justices disagreed with this reasoning and Justice Jackson in a dissent was sharply critical of the Court's opinion. He said:

The Court sustains this legislation by assuming two deviations from the facts of this particular case; first, it assumes a state of facts the record does not support, and secondly, it refuses to consider the facts which are inescapable on the record.[16]

Seldom has a justice of the Supreme Court so castigated a brother member's work, for one of the worst things one judge can say about the work of another is that he has "fudged on the facts." Yet it is hard to deny that there is something to be said in support of the criticism. The hypothesis which Justice Black's opinion assumed was that the township ordinance did no more than provide "a general program to help parents get their children, regardless of their religion, safely and expeditiously to and from accredited schools." [17] Actually the township did not furnish transportation, but reimbursed parents for what they had suffered from the fact that the township did not furnish it. Therefore the expenditure of public money had no effect upon the child's safety or expedition in transit.

The fact which Justice Black's opinion did not set forth was that the resolution which authorized the disbursement of the public money limited the reimbursement to parents whose children attended public and Catholic schools. The parents of those who attended non-Catholic private schools did not receive such aid. Thus, as Justice Jackson pointed out, children were classified according to the kinds of schools they attended.

Many observers saw in this decision a serious threat to the principle of complete separation of church and state. If transportation to a parochial school is to be paid, they argued, why might not the state likewise pay for the erection of a school building for citizens of a particular faith, and why, indeed, might it not pay the salaries of teachers in church schools when they are engaged in teaching the same subjects embraced in the public school curriculum? Organizations were formed to combat this tendency and a great deal of adverse criticism arose. Whether or not such criticism had anything to do with it, a year later there issued from Justice Black's pen a strong and forthright condemnation of a widespread effort that organized religions were making to use the facilities of the public-school system for religious teaching.[18]

HUGO L. BLACK

The case arose when a taxpayer and patron of an Illinois public school sought to prevent a school board from continuing a system under which sectarian groups were allowed to use the school building for the purpose of religious instruction during one period each week. No child was compelled to receive such instruction and the persons selected to give it, although chosen by the several sectarian groups, were subject to approval by the school superintendent. Regular classes were suspended in order that pupils whose parents requested it might be taught the faith and doctrine of a selected religion. Protestants and Catholics made the most of the opportunity to indoctrinate children who might otherwise not have come under their influence. The Jews tried it a while but abandoned the undertaking. Actually the method was a part of a plan of wide scope, promoted by the churches and making fast headway.[19]

The petitioner who raised the issue in the Illinois courts contended that the plan not only required the use of public school property for sectarian teaching but also constituted a perversion of the compulsory attendance statute in that it furnished the long arm of the law to rabbis, priests, and parsons to gather together an audience to whom they might preach their several creeds. Her personal grievance was that her child was humiliated and branded as a nonconformist, all because his mother did not desire that he be instructed in a faith in which she did not believe.

Justice Black thought her position well taken. Quoting the language of the Court in the Everson case he reiterated: "Neither a state nor the Federal Government can . . . pass laws which aid one religion, aid all religions, or prefer one religion over an-

158

other." [20] Justices Frankfurter, Jackson, Rutledge, and Burton who had dissented in the Everson case concurred but, in an opinion by Justice Frankfurter, called attention to their position in the former case which they thought indistinguishable in principle from the one at bar. Black is correct this time, they said in effect, but keep in mind that we have been saying this all along and that his wrong opinion is now answered by his right one. Black, for his part, admitted no necessity for any effort to reconcile the principles laid down in the two cases. The former he mentioned only to quote the broad principles there enunciated and to solidify into law what may there have been dictum. How the facts of the former case removed it from the law of the latter was not explained. Without assuming to predict his future course of conduct, it may be well to remember that Justice Black's honest recantation in the Gobitis case is some precedent for a change of mind.[21]

Justice Black's zeal for protecting personal liberty is equally intense when the freedoms involved are those of speech and press. In cases where the scope of these freedoms has been the issue, as in those concerning religious liberty, he has uniformly favored a broad interpretation of the constitutional guaranty against their infringement. An example of his earnest belief in the freedom of the press is furnished by a case in which such freedom was said to conflict with another constitutional right dear to his heart—that of a fair trial.[22]

While the trial of a member of the International Longshoremen and Warehousemen's Union was in progress Harry Bridges, the head of the union, published a telegram which he had dispatched to the Secretary of Labor, advising him that in the event the court decided an issue in a certain way, a strike would be called which would tie up shipping on the whole Pacific coast. While Bridges was doing this a metropolitan newspaper of strong anti-union sentiments printed an editorial saying that the trial judge would make a serious mistake if he granted probation to the defendant. Both Bridges and the newspaper were cited for criminal contempt and adjudged guilty.

When the case reached the Supreme Court Justice Black wrote the opinion which reversed the judgment of conviction. Adhering to the "clear and present danger" test, he declared that before such danger could operate to curb free speech, "the substantive evil must be extremely serious and the degree of imminence extremely high."[23] He did not believe that the possibility that the trial court could be influenced by outside threats or newspaper advice reached this superlative degree of importance.

Justice Frankfurter, with whom Chief Justice Stone and Justices Roberts and Byrnes agreed, dissented on the ground that one of the occasions when freedom of expression might properly be limited was when it was employed to influence improperly the course of a trial. In language which was almost a paraphrase of that which Black had used more than once he inveighed against narrowing a state's power to deal with local exigencies.

Justice Black was also in agreement with the opinion of the Court which held unconstitutional a Texas statute requiring labor organizers to register with the Secretary of State before they could conduct their business of soliciting union memberships.[24] It was insisted by Texas that since no tax was levied upon such activities and no discretion lodged in the Secretary of State with respect to

160

accepting registrations, compliance with the statute constituted no appreciable limitation upon free expression. Along with the majority of the Court, however, Justice Black thought the requirement that one must register before he undertook to make a public speech enlisting the support of any lawful movement was incompatible with the guaranties of free speech.

On two separate occasions Justice Black has denounced as unconstitutional sections of the Management Labor Relations Act, popularly known as the Taft-Hartley Act. The first case involved the constitutionality of the provision which made it unlawful for labor organizations to make contributions or expenditures in connection with the election of federal officers.[25] The Congress of Industrial Organizations promptly tested the validity of the prohibition by publishing and distributing a union periodical in which union members were urged to vote for a certain candidate for Congress. A district court dismissed the resulting indictment on the ground that the statute unjustifiably abridged the freedom of expression. On appeal by the Government, four members of the Supreme Court in an opinion by Justice Reed so construed the language of the statute that it did not pertain to the particular act for which the Congress of Industrial Organizations had been indicted. Justices Rutledge, Black, Douglas and Murphy, however, thought that the language of the statute was pertinent to the acts alleged in the indictment and that, because it denounced expenditures made for the expression of opinion, it contravened the provisions of the First Amendment.[26]

The second provision of the Taft-Hartley Act to call forth Justice Black's denunciation was the section withholding the advantages afforded by the statute from unions whose officers did not subscribe to a non-Communist affidavit. This affidavit must include the following pledges: first, that the officer is not a member of or affiliated with the Communist Party, and, secondly, that he is not a member of nor does he support any organization that believes in the overthrow of the United States Government by force or by any illegal and unconstitutional methods. Justice Black was the only justice to condemn this provision in its entirety. In his dissent he refused pointblank to compromise in any degree the principle that a man's political beliefs and affiliations belong beyond the pale of governmental interference and that any discrimination by law between citizens according to their beliefs and political connections is a dangerous intrusion upon personal liberty.[27]

The thread of the argument in the majority opinion written by Chief Justice Vinson was that, since for particular work persons from certain groups were likely to be ill suited, it was not an unlawful discrimination to exclude them from those to whom such work was assigned. It could hardly be called objectionable, he said, if members of the Secret Service force assigned to protect the person of the President were selected exclusively from those who did not believe in the President's assassination. So in the present case Congress might be permitted to say that in erecting a system in the interest of a free-flowing interstate commerce it would not depend on the cooperation of unions whose officers belonged to a group whose members desired to promote the kind of strikes which the system was being organized to prevent. Since Congress had reasonably found it to be a part of the Communist program to promote political strikes it could exclude from participation in the operation of the machinery intended to prevent such strikes those whose philosophy taught that they should be encouraged. The challenged section of the act, he said, was "designed to protect the public not against what Communists . . . advocate or believe, but against what Congress has concluded they have done and are likely to do again." [28]

With this view Justices Reed and Burton wholly agreed. Justices Frankfurter and Jackson concurred in part and dissented in part, and Justices Douglas, Clark, and Minton did not participate. Justice Frankfurter dissented on the ground that in some of the provisions of the section under review Congress had "cast its net too indiscriminately" and foresaw the danger of "mere speculation and uncertainty." Justice Jackson in a widely quoted opinion agreed with the Chief Justice that the provision requiring an affidavit to the effect that the officers were not members of the Communist Party was constitutional and seized upon the opportunity vigorously to denounce Communists and their tactics. Nevertheless, he found the second part of the requirement, that unions officers must swear that they did not *believe in communism*, invalid on the ground that no government under any circumstance has a right to "attempt foreclosure of any line of thought."

Justice Black alone held that the requirement of an oath concerning political affiliations, as well as one concerning political opinions, violated the Constitution. The decision of the Court, he insisted, rejected the fundamental constitutional principle that "beliefs are inviolate" and opened the way to compromise in "a field where the First Amendment forbids compromise." [29] Study of history had convinced him that no matter how rational and needful laws aimed at a political or religious group might seem at the moment of passage, their effect was inevitably to "generate hatreds and prejudices which rapidly spread beyond control." [30] The very heart of the American system, he said, is the postulate of the First Amendment—"that our free institutions can be maintained without proscribing or penalizing political belief, speech, press, assembly, or party affiliation" [31]—a luxury which despotic governments cannot afford.

As proof that his concern for the freedom of expression on political matters does not operate only when labor is involved is Justice Black's dissent from an opinion of the Court which upheld a section of the Hatch Act denouncing certain political activities on the part of federal employees.[32] As Black saw the matter the Constitution guaranteed to federal employees the same right that other citizens had to engage in political activities. Had the measure deprived five million farmers or five million business men of similar rights of participation in elections, he said, no one would question its illegality, and he could see no appreciable difference when the prohibition applied to civil servants. Any statute which would prevent "millions of citizens from contributing their arguments, complaints, and suggestions to the political debates which are the essence of our democracy," [33] seemed to Black clearly to violate the Constitution.

In cases involving charges of unconstitutional discrimination against members of the Negro race Justice Black has consistently insisted that the spirit of the constitutional requirement forbidding such discrimination be strictly observed, and he is unwilling to

164

permit compromises which evidence no more than token compliance. Where such cases have been based upon the denial of equal educational opportunities he has agreed with the majority of the Court that Negroes are entitled to admission to state supported universities unless the state provides similar and equal opportunities for its Negro citizens elsewhere.[34] Moreover, he has disapproved as improperly discriminatory a regulation that would set apart Negro students and compel them to occupy special seats in class rooms, libraries, and dining halls.[35]

Twice he has voted to overrule decisions of the Interstate Commerce Commission which allowed railroads to discriminate against Negroes in the use of Pullman and dining car facilities,[36] and he agreed with the majority of the Court that a statute of Virginia requiring Negro passengers on buses travelling in interstate commerce to move to the back of the bus when it crossed the Virginia state line placed an unconstitutional burden upon interstate commerce.[37] Also he joined the opinion of the Court which held that private agreements never to sell to persons of particular races were not enforceable in the courts.[38]

Yet despite his unquestioned devotion to the fundamental personal liberties, in time of national peril Justice Black has adopted the maxim, *"salus populi est suprema lex,"* and has voted to uphold governmental action which he admitted would be clearly unconstitutional under normal conditions. In the widely discussed case involving the right of the government to remove all persons of Japanese ancestry from the Pacific Coast as a matter of national defense,[39] Justice Black wrote the opinion of the Court upholding the power of the government to do so. The move of the military

165

was without precedent. A whole class of people, regardless of whether they were citizens or aliens, friends or foes, trusted or suspected, were uprooted from their homes and businesses and sent off to concentration camps.

Justice Black was careful to restate his opposition to racial discrimination, but pointed out that such discrimination was not *per se* unconstitutional. On the ground that desperate diseases may require desperate remedies he held that public safety transcended the protection of individual rights and property. Admitting that "compulsory exclusion of large groups of citizens from their homes, except under circumstances of direst emergency and peril," [40] is inconsistent with the Constitution, he nevertheless held that the emergency and peril had been at hand, or at any rate had seemed to be at hand, at the time of the military order and that the Government, because of danger reasonably apprehended, had acted within its constitutional authority.

In the light of this opinion it is difficult to see how any civil right may be expected to withstand a military emergency, if indeed any civil right has ever been able to do so. Justice Jackson, dissenting, expressed the opinion that while the courts should not attempt to interfere with the army in carrying out its task, neither should they be asked to lend their aid in executing a military expedient that had no place in law under the Constitution. Justice Murphy likewise dissented declaring that the exclusion order fell "into the ugly abyss of racism." [41]

Indicative of the fact that Justice Black's decision was not motivated by any war-engendered hostility to the Japanese race are several cases relating to the rights of Japanese in this country separated from the issue of national safety. He has voiced a vigorous opinion denouncing a California statute forbidding ownership of agricultural lands by aliens ineligible for citizenship on the ground that it denies to them the equal protection of the law as guaranteed by the Fourteenth Amendment,[42] and upon the same reasoning he struck down a California law which forbade the issuance of commercial fishing licenses to the same group.[43]

As might be expected from his disposition to place national safety above all other considerations, Justice Black has lent an attentive ear to accusations of treason even where they fell within a twilight zone of definition of that unique crime. The objective philosopher may be able to find no reason except the sovereign's own self interest for the odium that has always attached to treason and given it a separate superlative rank in the catalogue of crimes, but Justice Black disdains any academic argument that may seem to palliate the seriousness of the offense. For him treason remains where the king's judges long ago placed it, at the very top of the list of malefactions, overshadowing in its enormity the worst felonies. He is not disposed to treat lightly an accusation of treason even where the particular act alleged as its basis is of a somewhat equivocal character.

The case of Cramer v. United States[44] was of this nature. The defendant, a German by birth, but a naturalized citizen, responded one evening to a mysterious message and went to the Grand Central Railroad Station in New York. Whom should he find there but an old friend of his who had once lived in this country but had returned to Germany, embraced the Nazi cause, and been transported back to the United States by submarine to act as saboteur. Thereafter Cramer saw the man several times, took meals and drinks with him and accepted about two thousand dollars to keep for him until he should need it. For this he was convicted of treason in the district court, but the Supreme Court held that the overt acts he had committed were insufficient to meet the constitutional requirements for a conviction of this offiense.

Justices Douglas and Black would have sustained the judgment of the district court. They thought his "aid and comfort to the enemy" within the purview of the treason laws, pointing out that he had lied to the officers about his friend's identity and recent whereabouts and also about the money he had got from him. That the saboteur had been aided and comforted by having these falsehoods told in his behalf as well as by other accommodations the defendant had extended seemed to the dissenters enough basis for a conviction.

In a case which involved the cancellation of a certificate of naturalization Justice Black favored upholding the order of cancellation.[45] It was proved that a naturalized citizen of the United States had taken a prominent part in the activities of the German Bund and other Nazi organizations. The jury which convicted him was convinced that he had never been attached to the political principles of the United States, notwithstanding the fact that he had so sworn when he was naturalized. Justice Black voted with the majority of the Court to uphold the revocation of his citizenship but felt it necessary to add a few words of his own. He fully realized, he said, the dangers inherent in denaturalization and had the judgment "rested on petitioner's mere philosophical or political beliefs, expressed or unexpressed," he would have refused to sustain it. He believed, however, that the petitioner was "serving the German Government with the same fanatical zeal which motivated the saboteurs sent to the United States to wage war," [46] and thought that Congress had the power to provide for the cancellation of citizenship under such circumstances.

Despite the vigor with which Justice Black has fought to preserve certain of the fundamental personal liberties provided by the Bill of Rights, he has been less solicitous than the minority of his brethren of one such guaranty. Instances of search and seizure which other members of the Court have deemed unreasonable have not appeared so to the former prosecuting attorney and investigating committee chairman. Possibly, like the public generally, he is influenced by the fact that almost always when the provisions of the Fourth Amendment are before the court they have been invoked by some flagrant law violator who has been "caught with the goods" and interposes the defense of unlawful search as a last resort to escape conviction. Yet such a statement must carry the hypothetical qualification, for the cases in which he has differed with the Court on this subject have been borderline.

Moreover, as is usual in such cases, they have involved the freedom from unreasonable search only incidentally, as upon motions to suppress evidence so obtained, which issue, in the view of one respectable commentator,[47] is entirely collateral, and should not be entertained in a criminal trial where the primary question is no more than the guilt or innocence of the defendant but should be left to separate proceedings against those charged with infringement upon the asserted right. While Justice Black has not intimated an agreement with this view, it seems clear that he does not fear that the heavens will fall because some officer in pursuit of evidence has peered further than he is entitled to look without the authority conferred by a search warrant.

So when officers, upon information that a suspected person was engaged in the sale of counterfeit gasoline ration coupons, arrested and searched a third person found in the company of the suspect, Justice Black, along with Chief Justice Vinson, thought the evidence admissible against the third person, although the other members of the Court held to the contrary.[48] Also where federal narcotic agents detected the fumes of burning opium and followed their noses to ferret out the user and made a search of her room without a warrant, Justice Black, this time joined by Justices Vinson, Reed, and Burton dissented from an opinion which held the search unjustified.[49] Nor was he willing to concur when the Court, through an opinion by Justice Murphy, extended the rule against the admissibility of evidence obtained by unwarranted search, to exclude proof obtained incidental to an arrest for a felony committed in the presence of officers, where such officers had had an opportunity to obtain a search warrant but had neglected to do so.[50]

In later opinions, however, he has appeared less tolerant of questionable search and seizure than his earlier votes seemed to indicate. Although he had dissented in the Trupiano case[51] where the reasonableness of the search had been held to turn upon the officer's opportunity to obtain a search warrant, he later expressed himself as believing that the rule there announced should be treated as an adoption of judicial policy even though he had thought it not required by the Constitution.[52] The administration

170

of criminal justice, he added, would not be unduly handicapped by the application of the ruling and to overrule it would work more mischief than adhering to it. So also in Lustig *v.* United States[53] he was among the five justices who voted to suppress evidence which local police had obtained by an illegal search and later called to the attention of a Federal officer who had not himself been guilty of any wrongdoing.

Such is the record of Justice Black upon the matter of personal liberties. It can be fairly said to evidence a wholesome respect for their preservation. If in a few cases he has not supported their expansion, he has not joined in any decision that lessens their effectiveness when applied under ordinary conditions. Under extraordinary conditions, however, when national security in time of war has seemed the pre-eminent issue his practical nature has shown through the shell of theory to follow the maxim that puts public safety ahead of all other considerations.

CHAPTER X

ONE AMONG NINE

While it is true that a court can be understood only in terms of the individuals who compose it, it is likewise true that these individuals can be adequately appraised only within the framework of the institution. For no justice, however independent of spirit, operates within a vacuum completely unmindful of the behavior of his eight judicial brethren. Cases are rarely decided without the concurrence of a majority of the Court and no amount of wisdom or legal learning on the part of an individual judge will find its way into decisions unless the requisite number of his colleagues can be persuaded to concur with him. Any evaluation of Justice Black's judicial performance, therefore, must include some reference to the associates who enable him to write his opinions into law or frustrate his efforts as the case may be.

Since justices like other men possess emotions as well as intellects, it is often hard to determine with any degree of certainty why one reacts in a given way to another. Ideological differences are sometimes difficult to distinguish from personality clashes and, to further complicate the matter, what begins as one may end up as the other. Since both are important in shaping the course of the law neither can be neglected. Almost from the time it began to take shape the Roosevelt Court was distinguished by an unprecedented number of non-unanimous opinions.[1] The fact that seven of the justices were appointed by President Roosevelt and the other two by his Democratic successor has made this internal dissension all the more striking. The cartoonist who portrayed the new Court voting in unison at President Roosevelt's direction [2] proved to be a poor prophet.

Moreover, there early became noticeable within the Court a rather consistent and distinct division, high-lighted by statistical tables prepared periodically by Professor C. Hermann Pritchett of the University of Chicago undertaking to show in percentages how every justice has agreed or disagreed with each of his brethren both in gross and upon the several sets of subjects into which issues are customarily divided.[3] While there are rather obvious limitations (fully recognized and admitted by Professor Pritchett himself) upon the significance of any such quantitative analysis of judicial agreement, the studies served to indicate and advertise the factional groups into which the Court had separated and to identify the points where the stress and strain of differences were most likely to occur.

Given the fact that a Court appointed so largely by one President had fallen into this state of frequent disagreement, both academicians and journalists set to work to discover the source of the friction—a quest not yet concluded to the satisfaction of all. Certain students suggest the answer that the Roosevelt Court moved so rapidly into uncharted fields of ligitation that but few landmarks existed to point the way, leaving each explorer to depend on no more than his instinctive and individual sense of direction. The members of the New Deal Court, they reason, were actually more in agreement than were their predecessors in that they were unanimous in seeking a particular end while disputing about how to reach it.

Such reasoning, however, was generally too abstract for journalists—or, at least, for their readers—and many explained the
Court's divisions within a more simple—and sensational—
framework, that of personalities, a notion which the justices
themselves somewhat encouraged by the trenchant language and
sharp retort sometimes employed in their opinions. When Justice
Black, for example, termed a statement of Justice Frankfurter, "a
wholly gratuitous assertion," [4] or Justice Jackson, speaking of an
opinion written by Justice Murphy, said "I give up. Now I realize
fully what Mark Twain meant when he said, 'The more you explain it, the more I don't understand it,' " [5] the expressions were
headlined as confirmation of the rumors of ill feeling. Perhaps
reporters sent to cover Opinion Monday found it easier to snatch
phrases than to follow argument.

After a while it became widely accepted that the leaders of the
two factions upon the Court were Justices Black and Frankfurter.
In Justice Black's camp were Justices Douglas, Murphy, and Rutledge, while Justice Frankfurter was supported by Justice Jackson.
Until his death Chief Justice Stone was in fairly high agreement
with Frankfurter and Jackson and Chief Justice Vinson and Justice
Burton have veered definitely in this direction. Most nearly pre-
serving a state of neutrality was Justice Reed, but he, too, seemed
to lean slightly toward the Frankfurter-Jackson coalition.[6] Given
such a situation it is not surprising that the balance of power was
precarious. Since the Black wing needed only attract one vote in
order to constitute itself a majority, its strength was readily apparent. To offset this advantage, however, was the fact that Chief
Justice Vinson and Justices Burton and Reed all had a tendency
toward alignment with the Frankfurter-Jackson bloc.

During their first term on the Court together Justices Black and Frankfurter were in complete agreement, but by the term beginning October 1946 their percentage of agreement in non-unanimous decisions had dropped to 35. During this term Black's percentage of agreement with the other Justices was as follows: Murphy, 81; Rutledge, 72; Douglas, 68; Vinson, 56; Reed, 54; Burton, 53; Jackson, 40.[7] The pattern of the justices' alignments on specific issues can best be shown in tabular form. Out of data extracted from Professor Pritchett's compilations the following picture emerges.

Alignments of Justices in Percentages in Selected Groups of Cases (a)
(Only Non-Unanimous Decisions Are Considered)

For the Individual in Civil Liberties Cases	For the Defendant in Criminal Cases	For Labor	For the Right of a State to Tax or Regulate Business	For Upholding Rulings of Administrative Agencies
I	II	III	IV	V
Murphy (97%)	Murphy (90%)	Murphy (94%)	Black (92%)	Black (81%)
Rutledge (71)	Rutledge (90)	Black (93)	Murphy (85)	Murphy (76)
Black (68)	Black (65)	Rutledge (88)	Douglas (84)	Douglas (66)
Douglas (65)	Douglas (63)	Douglas (86)	Frankfurter (79)	Rutledge (67)
Stone (44)	Stone (44)	Reed (66)	Stone (74)	Burton (67)
Jackson (33)	Frankfurter (39)	Jackson (52)	Reed (59)	Reed (67)
Reed (32)	Jackson (28)	Frankfurter (44)	Rutledge (58)	Jackson (62)
Roberts (32)	Reed (27)	Stone (32)	Burton (33)	Frankfurter (61)
Frankfurter (29)	Roberts (27)	Burton (32)	Jackson (31)	Vinson (50)
Burton (17)	Burton (16)	Vinson (27)	Vinson (13)	Stone (51)
Vinson (0)	Vinson (0)	Roberts (5)	Roberts (13)	Roberts (14)

(a) These statistics are taken from *The Roosevelt Court,* pp. 89, 131, 162, 190, 208. Column I is based on the 1939-1946 terms of the Court. Column IV is based on the 1938-1946 terms. The remainder are based on the 1941-1946 terms.

From this table it is apparent that Justice Black yielded to none in his determination to uphold the power of the states to tax and regulate business as they see fit. Similarly he was the justice most likely to approve the rulings of federal administrative agencies. In the defense of civil liberties he lagged behind both Justices Murphy and Rutledge, and behind Justice Murphy in his support of labor. It is interesting to note that Justice Frankfurter slipped into the liberal ranks in cases wherein the right of a state to regulate business was involved. He demanded the greatest possible freedom for the states, not only in economic matters, but also in the realm of civil liberties. In the latter category of cases he upheld the power of the state against the individual 71 per cent of the time and in cases involving state regulation of business he was on the side of the state 79 per cent of the time. Justice Black, on the other hand, was willing to uphold the states in 92 per cent of the cases where they were attempting to regulate business, but voted for them only 32 per cent of the time when they were imposing restraints or qualifications upon individual civil liberties.

Some of the disciples of Frankfurter began to question Black's intellectual honesty, and charge that he did not scruple to use constitutional principles first one way and then the other to suit the end he desired to attain in particular cases. Concerning Frankfurter, on the other hand, admirers of Black cried "Ichabod," and considered him a deserter from the liberal ranks. Furthermore, said many, from the time of his appointment he had been a marplot and a breeder of faction who continued to play back-stage politics even after his elevation to the Court. There is some evidence that this last charge is based upon reality. For example, Harold Ickes declared that it was Frankfurter who prevented his being offered the War Portfolio at the time of Stimson's appointment.[8]

While most observers thought Black and Frankfurter the leading antagonists upon the Court, there were some who asserted that this feud was a secondary one and that the real contest was between Douglas and Frankfurter who, according to back-step gossip, thoroughly distrusted each other. Still others thought the real trouble lay between Douglas and Jackson, the two members of the Court suspected of harboring further political ambitions. Both had been mentioned as presidential and vice-presidential candidates and neither had indicated that the suggestions were unwelcome. A few even thought that Jackson's hostility to the Black wing was really prompted by a dislike of Murphy dating back to their days of association in the Department of Justice. Such disparity of conjecture meant that little was actually known about the origin of the factions, but what was agreed upon and currently accepted as a fact was that factions existed and that they were not wholly the result of idealistic division. Whatever the cause, all was not well with the personal relations of the justices.

It was Justice Jackson who finally dragged out into the open proof that fire actually existed behind the smoke of rumor. Except for him, succeeding years might have covered the personal discord with the grass of forgetfulness and future historians would hardly have credited tales that they could not document. Justice Jackson, however, changed all this and in an unprecedented attack upon

Justice Black pulled back the curtain of discretion and exposed in ugly detail the factionalism with which the Court was beset.

The occasion of the explosion was the vacancy which occurred in the office of Chief Justice in 1946 upon the death of Chief Justice Stone. From the White House came word that his successor would be named from among the present members of the Court[9] and almost everyone thought this meant Justice Jackson who was then in Nürnberg as Chief American Prosecutor at the German War Criminals Trial. He had been mentioned for the post even before the death of Chief Justice Stone and, according to one of Roosevelt's cabinet members, he had been seriously considered for the place at the time Stone had been selected and had been disappointed then that he had not been named.[10] When he was later offered a subordinate place upon the Court he had asked a friend to go to President Roosevelt and find out whether acceptance would stand in the way of his appointment to the Chief Justiceship when next a vacancy occurred. The President replied that it would not and under these circumstances Justice Jackson's hopes mounted high.[11] Although a new President occupied the White House when Chief Justice Stone died, he was the deceased President's selection and Justice Jackson probably expected him to carry out what he thought was his predecessor's purpose.

When the President unexpectedly appointed Secretary of the Treasury Fred Vinson to the coveted position Justice Jackson broke all restraints of etiquette and precedent and exposed his rage and disappointment to an astonished people. In a public letter to the Senate and House Judiciary Committees he declared that the time had come for Congress to have the facts concerning the long-rumored "feud" to which he was a party. It had been reported to him, he said, that in his absence one of his colleagues had made "publicized threats to the President," which had been "exploited through certain inspired commentators and columnists to imply that offensive behavior" on his part was responsible for what he termed "the feud on the Court." [12]

The article that Justice Jackson referred to as having "publicized threats to the President" was one by Doris Fleeson in the Washington *Star* [13] in which she purported to tell the inside story of the "Jackson-Black Battle." President Truman was quoted as having said, "Black says he will resign if I make Jackson Chief Justice and tell the reason why. Jackson says the same thing about Black." Later President Truman denied that he had ever discussed the pending appointment with any member of the Court,[14] and, of course, the quotation was never authenticated. However, by the time President Truman made this statement the damage was done. Justice Jackson had been in no humor to wait for proof. Notoriously high-tempered and given to impulsive action when enraged, he lashed out at Justice Black whom he obviously blamed for his failure to receive the coveted appointment and made public his side of the controversy which had accentuated his ill feeling.

According to Jackson's statement, Black had become very angry with him over an opinion which he had attached to a formal dismissal of a petition for rehearing[15] and had threatened "open warfare" if Jackson insisted upon leaving it in the reports. "I told him that I would not stand for anymore of his bullying," said Jackson, "and that I would now have to write my opinion to keep self-respect in the face of threats."

179

The case that brought about the declaration of war was one which involved the issue of portal-to-portal pay for miners.[16] Justice Murphy, writing for a majority of five justices including Black, held the coal miners entitled to pay for the time it took them to go from the opening of the mine to the spot where they began their actual work. Justice Jackson wrote a dissent in which Chief Justice Stone, Justice Frankfurter, and Justice Roberts joined.

Then came a petition for a rehearing upon grounds perhaps not unique but at any rate so unusual that a similar situation is not revealed among the annotations of the countless cases in which disappointed lawyers have employed this means to say a last word before the court's adverse judgment is finally executed. Although judicial expression gives no countenance to the theory, judges often remark off the record that the chief purpose served by petitions to rehear is to give unsuccessful attorneys an opportunity to "blow off steam" in a sort of dignified manner and to show their clients that they went down fighting even to their last gasp. All of which is to say that petitions to rehear are seldom filed hopefully, and far more seldom, successfully.

What went on in the councils of the lawyers for the mine operators after the portal-to-portal decision can only be guessed, but of this much we can be pretty certain: the petition was not filed with much hope that it would bring about a change in the Court's judgment. There was no room in precedent or reason for the lodgment of such optimism. What it did furnish was the opportunity to criticize Justice Black and attack his ideas of judicial propriety because he had not recused himself when one of his former law partners appeared to argue the case for the miners. For this reason the petition for rehearing asked that the judgment be annulled.

Seven justices thought that this petition for rehearing should be disposed of in the usual manner by a mere notation that it was denied. Justices Jackson and Frankfurter, however, felt called upon to attach a statement to the denial, innocent enough on its face, but couched in language which carefully avoided any connotation that they themselves would have done as Black did and hinting that it was lack of authority which prevented them from censuring Black's conduct. The propriety of withdrawing in any particular circumstance rested with the individual justices, they pointed out, and there was no authority "under which the majority of this Court has power under any circumstances to exclude one of its duly commissioned justices from sitting or voting in any case." [17] The opinion made no mention of the custom that supported Black's course, an omission that probably left in Black's mind a rather reasonable suspicion that its purpose had not been friendly. Justice Jackson's later fulmination left little doubt that such suspicion was justified. In his explanatory letter Jackson maintained that he had never charged Black with lack of honor, but that he had merely questioned "his judgment as to sound judicial policy" in adopting a course that would if followed "soon bring the Court into disrepute." In a final display of bad taste he concluded: "I want that practice stopped. If it is ever repeated while I am on the bench I will make my Jewell Ridge opinion look like a letter of recommendation by comparison."

What the enraged Justice meant to accomplish by his outburst is difficult to see: what he did accomplish, easy. Immediately throughout the country politicians, newspaper writers, and lawyers took sides in the controversy or equally condemned both justices. Undoubtedly the Court had now been brought "into disrepute" in many quarters. Some who had been hostile to Black from the beginning took occasion to justify their previous judgment. Always anti-Black, the New York *Herald Tribune* called for the resignation of both Black and Jackson, declaring that the usefulness of each was now ended. "It hardly seems possible," said this newspaper,

that Justice Black, a man who many believe should never have been appointed in the first place, can survive the accusations brought against him. It is hoped . . . that this will prove the last of the misfortunes which we have inherited from President Roosevelt's light-hearted jugglings with the judicial process.[18]

Also crying "a plague on both your houses," the New York *Times* declared that Justice Jackson had committed an error of taste, but that Justice Black had committed the worse offense of lowering judicial standards.[19]

Senator Scott Lucas demanded the resignations of both men in order "to preserve the integrity of the Supreme Court," [20] and Senator Styles Bridges implored his colleagues in the Senate to define the term "good behavior" as employed in the constitutional provision that judges "shall hold office during good behavior." [21] A joint resolution was introduced in the Senate proposing a constitutional amendment that would limit to three the number of justices any one president might appoint and which would remove Justices Douglas, Murphy, Jackson, and Rutledge by retroactive provision.[22]

Justice Black did not find himself without friends. Most liberal writers came to his defense, among whom were many who had bitterly criticized his appointment nine years before. Most of them attributed Jackson's outburst to no more than bad temper and pique over having missed a coveted honor, and others pointed out that there was ample precedent to justify the course which Black had followed. Marshall Field's newspaper, *P.M.*, found a parallel for Jackson's attitude in that of the "G.I. who grows resentful against those 'damn civilians' across the ocean." [23] The *New Republic* pointed out that those who condemned Black were the conservatives who hated him for his liberal views and were always on the lookout for some opportunity to smear him.[24] Arthur Schlesinger, Jr. offered a psychological explanation for Jackson's conduct, declaring it "the act of a weary and sorely beset man, committed to a harassing task in a remote land, tormented by the certainty that the chief justiceship had now passed forever out of his reach." Jackson's revelations had done nothing to shake Schlesinger's judgment that Black was "an honorable person, not given to petty politicking." [25] Harold Ickes, who professed friendship for both men, thought that Jackson "in a particularly unhappy frame of mind because he failed to get the appointment he coveted," had erroneously ascribed to Black the opposition to his appointment.[26]

To the everlasting credit of Justice Black's good sense and self-control, he made no reply to Justice Jackson's charge. Reporters who besieged him for a statement were accorded no more than a disappointing "no comment." Although it did not require much discernment to know that it would be execrable taste to reply to Jackson's diatribes in like manner, there must have been a temptation to answer questioners by saying that judicial ethics and propriety forbade such a course, thereby adding some additional heat to the water in which Justice Jackson found himself. Justice Black, however, elected to remain silent, and so contributed to the preservation of both his own dignity and that of the Court.

Certainly it does not appear either from the record or from outside explanations that Justice Black had in any measure abused his office or even followed a course that lacked ample precedent. Highly respected justices have often sat in cases in which their former law partners appeared as counsel, as well as those in which former clients were involved as litigants.[27] To many it would appear that a justice's refusal to do so smacks of pious pretense rather than a true fear that feeling might bias judgment. Moreover, one need only to examine Black's record to be convinced that in the Jewell Ridge case he was voting just the way his previous judicial course would have indicated. Justice Jackson himself was careful to say that he did not impugn Black's honor, yet in spite of this disavowal it was certain from the beginning what interpretation would be given the statement and it cannot be doubted that Jackson was well aware of this at the time of its utterance.

Wherein lay the roots of his personal animus toward Black can hardly be more than a matter of conjecture. It is unlikely that it began only when Black angrily said that a separate opinion of Jackson and Frankfurter upon the petition for a rehearing in the Jewell Ridge case meant "open war." Indeed the very use of the term indicated that an undeclared war was already in progress.

Also it is unlikely that Jackson would have insisted upon appending a separate opinion had his consideration of law and policy been wholly unmixed with personal mistrust and dislike. By the same token this animosity must have been ready to be fanned into fury at the time of his disappointment in Nürnberg. Obviously his rage was something more than a sudden and spontaneous outbreak. Somewhere along the line Justice Black had given him deep offense, deep enough to make him subject to a fit of temper and its consequent indiscretion.

While one would not be justified in ascribing to Justice Black, merely on the basis of this incident, a want of that conciliatory and deferential nature that holds personal antagonisms to a minimum, there are other indications that despite his surface amiability his uncompromising and aggressive promotion of causes which enlist his sympathy often irritates and angers those with whom he differs. As a senator he aroused active enmities among some of his colleagues and his judicial career has been beset by like difficulties.

Whether this unfortunate characteristic played a part in driving the wedge between the two wings of the Court is impossible of determination. It cannot be denied that certain of the justices indulged in a good deal of sniping at one another in their opinions, and it seems highly probable that much of this undignified behavior was prompted by personal animosities. On the other hand, there is little or no evidence to warrant the conclusion that any one of the justices allowed his feelings toward his colleagues to influence his ultimate decisions. Nevertheless, since justices have sometimes shown themselves to be "all too human" the possibility that personality clashes may occasionally influence the course of the law requires the examination of such factors.

With the deaths of Justices Murphy and Rutledge in the summer of 1949 the once powerful coalition of liberals, Black, Douglas, Murphy, and Rutledge, was dissolved. Added to this Justice Douglas failed to participate in many decisions of the 1949-1950 term because of an injury sustained in an accident, thus leaving Black alone to voice the views they might have supported. His isolation was reflected by the large number of sole dissents which he wrote—more than twice the number written by any other justice.[28]

The Jackson-Frankfurter alignment continued and, surprisingly enough, Justice Black not infrequently joined them in dissent, accompanying them in minority opinions more often than he so accompanied others.[29] It is still too early to fit Justices Clark and Minton into any pattern, not only because of the short period of time they have served, but also because they have failed to participate in the consideration of many important cases. There is no indication, however, that they veer in the direction of Justice Black. Not once has Justice Clark joined him in dissent and Justice Minton has dissented in his company only once. Thus the influence of Justice Black's judicial philosophy upon the course of constitutional development may reasonably be expected to decline in the immediate future.

CONCLUSION

The foregoing survey of Justice Black's public career warrants the assertion that the fountainhead of his political philosophy is a desire to improve the lot of the common man and protect him from the oppression of powerful forces. Toward the attainment of this end he would employ the instruments of government to effect far-reaching social and economic reforms, completely rejecting the thesis that the government governs best which governs least. Therefore he accords to government, whether it be state or national, the widest latitude when it appears to be working in the interest of the little man and he is impatient of legal concepts which halt legislative action in behalf of the general welfare.

When the economically powerful come before the Supreme Court contending that by some tax or regulation they have been deprived of their property without due process of law or that their activities are immune from public regulation because of relation to interstate commerce they receive scant sympathy from Black who generally votes to uphold the power of the government. Moreover, that a number of individuals should be allowed to associate themselves together and demand that their group interest be treated as that of a single citizen does not seem to Black a corollary to the proposition of equality before the law. To him it appears reasonable that a number of men acting jointly may justly be burdened with rules and regulations against which individual activity is protected, and he regards it as presumptuous when such associates demand that their organization be regarded as a person endued with all the rights which the Constitution sought to save for men of flesh and blood.

Despite Justice Black's belief in positive government he is by no means willing to sanction all governmental action, and when it is a government rather than some private person or association of persons that moves in a manner which seems to him to disadvantage the common man he strikes at it quite as vigorously. When the Interstate Commerce Commission appeared to favor a class of carriers at the expense of the consuming public, the fact that it was an arm of the government gave it no position of advantage before Black, although he had persistently pled with his brethren to keep judicial hands off other governmental agencies whose actions he believed to be in the public interest.

Likewise when a government acts in such a way as appears to him to deny to some individual citizen one of his rights or liberties guaranteed by the Constitution he does not hesitate to censure such action. Particularly zealous has he been to protect the freedoms of speech, press, and religion. The right to trial by jury is in his mind no outmoded process to be whittled away by exceptions and restrictions. So devoted is he to the several provisions of the Bill of Rights that he has conducted a judicial crusade to have them held applicable to the states as well as to the federal government, a sharper break with precedent than he has yet persuaded the Court to take.

Yet for all his sympathy with the little man Black is no sentimentalist and his feelings seldom cloud his common sense. When it appears that the little man has in reality had a fair deal he is ready to let the law take its course, and when national safety seems at stake he is willing to sacrifice personal liberties.

CONCLUSION

Probably in the Court's whole history no member has shown less compunction than has Justice Black in departing from judicial precedent. With such legal philosophers as Justice Cardoza and Professor Williston he believes that when a rule is found to be "inconsistent with the sense of justice or with the social welfare" it should be immediately and frankly destroyed rather than allowed to wash away through continued erosion.[1] The great emphasis which courts lay upon settled law and the abhorrence which they so often express for judicial legislation have made small impression upon Black.

He is charged with ignoring legal principles in order to decide each case in accord with his own views of rightness, and it must be admitted that he appears to regard such principles as flexible when his views of rightness demand a variation. Undoubtedly he conceives the Court to be but another instrument of democracy, forged for the same purpose as the legislative and executive branches and having no reason for its existence other than the promotion of general welfare. Technicalities which stand in the way of this accomplishment are to be removed at the earliest opportunity—and removed by the Court itself if placed in the law by judicial interpretation.

It is probable that Justice Black belongs to that school of thought which holds that every judge, consciously or unconsciously, writes into his opinions his own economic, social, and political ideas and that the notion of judicial impartiality is little more than a myth. At any rate he has gone to no pains to disguise the fact that he himself has positive ideas of rightness which he believes should be embodied in the law and when he incorporates these in his opinions he feels little necessity for apology or rationalization. Perhaps he no more than others writes his feelings into law, but does so more candidly.

History has now gone far enough to allow no doubt of Justice Black's learning and ability. No one ever doubted his intellectual energy. By dint of these qualities directed in behalf of the common man and grounded upon a faith in the possibility of just and efficient democratic government, he has earned a unique distinction among those who have held membership upon the Supreme Court.

NOTES

NOTES TO CHAPTER I

[1] Although this statement does not appear in the *United States Reports,* Justice McReynolds made it orally when handing down his dissent in the Gold Clause Cases, 294 U. S. 361 (1934). For the full text of his remarks upon that occasion see, "Justice McReynolds' Dissent in the Gold Clause Cases," *Tennessee Law Review* (June, 1945), XVIII, 768.

[2] Drew Pearson and Robert S. Allen, *The Nine Old Men* (New York, 1936), Chap. IV.

[3] Norman *v.* Baltimore and Ohio Railroad Co., 294 U. S. 240 (1935); Perry *v.* United States, 294 U. S. 330 (1935).

[4] A. L. A. Schechter Corporation *v.* United States, 295 U. S. 495 (1935).

[5] Railroad Retirement Board *v.* Alton Railroad Co., 295 U. S. 330 (1935).

[6] Louisville Joint Stock Land Bank *v.* Radford, 295 U. S. 555 (1935).

[7] Carter *v.* Carter Coal Co., 298 U. S. 238 (1936).

[8] United States *v.* Butler, 297 U. S. 1 (1936).

[9] *Ex parte* McCardle, 7 Wallace 506 (1869).

[10] H. Doc. No. 142, 75th Cong., 1st sess.

[11] Malcolm R. Patterson of Tennessee in 1910.

[12] For a detailed account of this struggle see Joseph Alsop and Turner Catledge, *The 168 Days* (New York, 1938).

[13] *Congressional Record,* August 12, 1937, p. 8732.

[14] *Newsweek,* August 21, 1937, p. 7.

[15] Senate, Special Committee on Investigation of Air Mail and Ocean Mail Contracts, *Hearings,* 73rd Cong., 2d sess.; Senate, Special Committee to Investigate Lobbying Activities, *Hearings,* 74th Cong., 1st and 2d sess.

[16] New York *Herald Tribune,* August 13, 1937.

[17] Washington *Post,* August 13, 1937.

[18] Birmingham *Age-Herald,* August 13, 1937.

[19] New York *Times,* August 15, 1937.

[20] Philadelphia *Record,* August 13, 1937.

[21] New York *Times,* August 15, 1937.

[22] "An Inquisitor Comes to Glory," *Newsweek,* August 21, 1937, p. 40.

[23] *New Republic,* August 25, 1937, p. 60.

[24] "Salute to Justice Black," *Nation,* August 21, 1937, p. 183.

[25] Paul S. Blakely, *The America,* August 28, 1937, p. 484.

[26] "Black of Alabama," *Commonweal,* August 27, 1937, p. 409.

[27] Baltimore *Afro-American,* August 21, 1937.

[28] *Ibid.*

[29] New York *Times,* August 21, 1937.

[30] For his full argument see *Congressional Record,* August 16, 1937, p. 8951 *et seq.*

[31] *Congressional Record,* August 17, 1937, p. 9069.

[32] *Ibid.,* p. 9097.

NOTES TO CHAPTER II

[1] Robert S. Allen, "Who Exposed Black?" *Nation*, September 25, 1937, p. 311.
[2] New York *Times*, September 13, 1937.
[3] *Ibid.*, September 17, 1937.
[4] *Ibid.*, September 19, 1937.
[5] *Ibid.*, September 30, 1937.
[6] *Ibid.*
[7] *Ibid.*
[8] *Editor and Publisher*, October 2, 1937.
[9] New York *Times*, October 2, 1937.
[10] New York *Herald Tribune*, October 3, 1937.
[11] New York *Times*, October 3, 1937.
[12] Boston *Post*, October 3, 1937.
[13] New Haven *Journal Courier*, October 3, 1937.
[14] Washington *Post*, October 3, 1937.
[15] Albany *Knickerbocker News*, October 3, 1937.
[16] Cleveland *News*, October 3, 1937.
[17] Chicago *Tribune*, October 3, 1937.
[18] Chatanooga *Times*, October 3, 1937.
[19] Columbia *Record*, October 3, 1937.
[20] Dallas *News*, October 3, 1937.
[21] New York *Sun*, October 3, 1937.
[22] Washington *Post*, October 3, 1937.
[23] "A Klansman on the Court," *New Republic*, October 13, 1937, p. 256.
[24] "Bigger than Black," *Nation*, September 25, 1937, p. 308.
[25] Albert J. Nock, "The Packing of Hugo Black," *American Mercury*, October, 1937, p. 229.
[26] Al Segal, *"Sic Transit,"* Baltimore *Jewish Times*, October 1, 1937, p. 31.
[27] "Talent Rewarded," *Catholic World*, November, 1937, p. 129.
[28] Information obtained from the Office of Public Opinion Research, Princeton University.
[29] *Ibid.*
[30] *Fortune*, January, 1938, p. 92.
[31] *Ex parte* Albert Levitt, 302 U. S. 633 (1937).

NOTES TO CHAPTER III

[1] This term is employed in the deep South to designate a member of a class rather than to describe an individual.

[2] New York *Times,* August 15, 1937.

[3] For a full explanation and defense of this bill see an article by Black, "The Shorter Work Week and Work Day," *Annals of the American Academy of Political Science* (March, 1936), CLXXXIV, 62-67.

[4] *Time,* April 17, 1933, p. 12.

[5] See his speech delivered before the American Association for Social Security on Desember 15, 1934, *Vital Speeches* (January 14, 1935), I, 249.

[6] Senate Bill No. 2176, 74th Cong., 1st sess.

[7] United States *v.* Butler, 297 U. S. 1 (1936).

[8] New York *Times,* August 15, 1936.

[9] For the full text of this speech see *Vital Speeches* (September 1, 1937), III, 674.

NOTES TO CHAPTER IV

[1] Senate, Special Committee on Investigation of Air Mail and Ocean Mail Contracts, *Hearings,* 73rd Cong., 2d sess., p. 1439 ff.

[2] New York *Times,* January 20, 1934.

[3] *Hearings* on Air Mail and Ocean Mail Contracts, pp. 1477 ff.

[4] New York *Times,* February 17, 1934.

[5] *Ibid.,* February 25, 1934.

[6] *Time,* March 5, 1934, p. 46.

[7] In addition interlocking directorates were prohibited as well as the selling and transferring of contracts without the consent of the Postmaster General. Bidders were required to submit a list of stockholders and directors together with a statement of their corporation's financial structure.

[8] *Time,* March 26, 1934, p. 55.

[9] *Hearings* on Air Mail and Ocean Mail Contracts, pp. 2112-2119.

[10] See Jurney *v.* McCracken, 294 U. S. 125 (1935).

[11] *Time,* July 22, 1935, p. 15.

[12] *Ibid.*

[13] New York *Times,* July 11, 1935.

[14] Senate, Special Committee to Investigate Lobbying Activities, *Hearings,* 74th Cong., 1st sess., p. 24.

[15] *Ibid.,* pp. 816-817.

[16] *Ibid.,* p. 1091.

[17] *Ibid.,* pp. 61-62.

[18] *Ibid.,* p. 65.

[19] *Ibid.,* p. 67.

[20] *Time,* August 5, 1935, p. 7.

[20] New York *Times,* August 15, 1935.

Notes to Chapter IV

[21] *Hearings* on Lobbying Activities, p. 1001.

[22] *Time,* March 16, 1936, p. 17.

[23] *Congressional Record,* March 5, 1936, p. 3330.

[24] New York *Times,* March 11, 1936.

[25] *Ibid.,* March 12, 1936.

[26] *Harper's Magazine,* February, 1936, p. 275.

[27] *Hearings* on Lobbying Activities, p. 1628.

NOTES TO CHAPTER V

[1] Connecticut General Life Insurance Co. *v.* California, 303 U. S. 77 (1938).

[2] McCart *v.* Indianapolis Water Co., 302 U. S. 419 (1938).

[3] New York Life Insurance Co. *v.* Gamer 303 U. S. 161 (1938).

[4] The following table is submitted for the purpose of comparison.

	Total Dissents	Lone Dissents
Hughes	0	0
McReynolds	26	4
Brandeis	1	0
Sutherland	9	0
Butler	20	1
Stone	5	0
Roberts	3	0
Cardozo	4	0
Black	16	12
Reed	2	1

[5] Federal Trade Commission *v.* Standard Education Society, 302 U. S. 112 (1937).

[6] *Ibid.,* p. 116.

[7] *Ibid.*

[8] McCart *v.* Indianapolis Water Co., 302 U. S. 419 (1938).

[9] 169 U. S. 466.

[10] *Ibid.,* p. 526.

[11] *Ibid.,* p. 546.

[12] *Ibid.,* p. 547.

[13] William E. Mosher, *Electrical Utilities: The Crisis in Public Control* (New York, 1929), p. 13.

[14] New York Commission on Revision of the New York Public Service Commission Law, *Hearings,* I, 381.

[15] Leon Jourolmon, "Life and Death of Smyth *v.* Ames," *Tennessee Law Review* (June, 1944), XVIII, 353.

[16] It was not until 1944, however, that the majority of the Court finally overruled Smyth *v.* Ames in Federal Power Commission *v.* Hope Natural Gas Co., 320 U. S. 591. For a history of judicial review of rate making see Leon Jourolmon,

"Life and Death of Smyth *v.* Ames, *Tennessee Law Review* (June, 1944), XVIII, 347; (April, 1945), XVIII, 663; (June, 1945), XVIII, 756.

[17] McCart *v.* Indianapolis Water Co., 302 U. S. 419, 428-429 (1938).

[18] *Ibid.,* p. 441.

[19] "Mr. Justice Black's First Year," *New Republic,* June 8, 1938, p. 118.

[20] 303 U. S. 77 (1938).

[21] It is claimed that the word "person" was substituted for the original "citizen" in order to extend the Amendment's protection to corporations. See Louis B. Boudin, "Truth and Fiction about the Fourteenth Amendment," *New York University Law Quarterly Review* (November, 1938), XVI, 19; Howard J. Graham, "The 'Conspiracy Theory' of the Fourteenth Amendment," *Yale Law Journal* (January, 1938), XLVII, 371 and (December, 1938), XLVIII, 171; Andrew C. McLaughlin, "The Court, the Corporation, and Conkling," *American Historical Review* (October, 1940), XLVI, 45.

[22] Charles A. Beard, *The Rise of American Civilization* (2 vols., New York, 1930), II, 114.

[23] 118 U. S. 394.

[24] *Ibid.,* p. 396.

[25] Connecticut General Life Insurance Co. *v.* Johnson, 303 U. S. 77, 85-86 (1938).

[26] *Ibid.,* p. 90.

[27] Marquis Childs, "The Supreme Court Today," *Harper's Magazine,* May, 1938, p. 581.

[28] 16 Peters 1.

[29] Erie Railroad*v.* Tompkins, 304 U. S. 64, 84 (1938).

[30] Black and White Taxicab and Transfer Co. *v.* Brown and Yellow Taxicab and Transfer Co., 276 U. S. 518, 535 (1928).

[31] New York Life Insurance Co. *v.* Gamer, 303 U. S. 161 (1938).

[32] *Ibid.,* p. 173.

[33] 303 U. S. 95 (1938).

[34] *Ibid.,* p. 109.

[35] J. D. Adams Manufacturing Co. *v.* Storen, 304 U. S. 307 (1938).

[36] "The Supreme Court Today," *Harper's Magazine,* May, 1938, p. 581.

[37] "Justice Black Dissenting," *Nation,* March 5, 1938, p. 264.

[38] New York *Times,* April 27, 1938.

[39] "Mr. Justice Black's First Year," *New Republic* June 8, 1938, p. 118.

[40] "Mr. Justice Black," *National Lawyers Guild Quarterly* (June, 1938), I, 181.

NOTES TO CHAPTER VI

[1] See International Shoe Company *v.* Washington, 326 U. S. 310 (1945).

[2] New York, 1944.

[3] Williams *v.* Standard Oil Co. of Louisiana, 278 U. S. 235 (1929).

[4] Nebbia *v.* New York, 291 U. S. 502 (1934).

[5] Hurtado *v.* California, 110 U. S. 516 (1884).

[6] Powell *v.* Alabama, 287 U. S. 45 (1932).

[7] 305 U. S. 434 (1939).

[8] *Ibid.,* p. 440.

[9] 322 U. S. 327 (1944).

[10] See Thomas Reed Powell, "Sales and Use Taxes: Collection from Absentee Vendors," *Harvard Law Review* (September, 1944), LVII, 1086-1097; William B. Lockhart, "The Sales Tax in Interstate Commerce," *Harvard Law Review* (February, 1939), LII, 617-644.

[11] For other cases in which Black followed a similar line of reasoning see, McCarroll *v.* Dixie Greyhound Lines, 309 U. S. 176 (1940); International Shoe Co. *v.* Washington, 326 U. S. 310 (1945); Hooven and Allison Co. *v.* Evatt, 324 U. S. 652 (1945).

[12] 305 U. S. 5 (1938).

[13] Southern Pacific Co. *v.* Arizona, 325 U. S. 761 (1945).

[14] *Ibid.,* p. 784.

[15] Indiana *ex rel.* Anderson *v.* Brand, 303 U. S. 95 (1938).

[16] 313 U. S. 362 (1941).

[17] Home Building and Loan Association *v.* Blaisdell, 290 U. S. 398 (1934).

[18] Wood *v.* Lovett, 313 U. S. 362, 383 (1941).

[19] McDougall *v.* Green, 335 U. S. 281 (1948).

[20] South, *v.* Peters, 70 S. Ct. 641 (1950).

[21] *Ibid.,* p. 643.

[22] The one exception has been the Interstate Commerce Commission with whose rulings Black has often been in sharp disagreement. See below pp. 99-100.

[23] 306 U. S. 240 (1939).

[24] *Ibid.,* p. 253.

[25] *Ibid.,* p. 267.

[26] For a discussion of this case see Henry M. Hart and Edward F. Pritchard, "The Fansteel Case: Employee Misconduct and the Remedial Powers of the National Labor Relations Board," *Harvard Law Review* (June, 1939), LII, 1275-1329.

[27] Southern Steamship Co. *v.* National Labor Relations Board, 316 U. S. 31 (1942).

[28] For other instances in which Black voted to uphold the power of the National Labor Relations Board see, National Labor Relations Board v. Indiana and Michigan Electric Company, 318 U. S. 9 (1943); National Labor Relations Board *v.* Falk Corporation, 308 U. S. 453 (1940); Wallace Corporation *v.* National Labor Relations Board, 323 U. S. 248 (1944).

[29] See, for example, his opinions in Fashion Originators' Guild *v.* Federal Trade Commission, 312 U. S. 457 (1940) and Federal Trade Commission *v.* Cement Institute, 333 U. S. 683 (1948); his concurring opinions in Federal Power Commission *v.* Natural Gas Pipeline Company, 315 U. S. 575 (1942) and Federal Power Commission *v.* Hope Natural Gas Company, 320 U. S. 591 (1944); his dissents in Federal Trade Commission *v.* Bunte Brothers, 312 U. S. 349 (1940);

Federal Power Commission *v.* Panhandle Eastern Pipe Line Co., 337 U. S. 498 (1949).

[30] Interstate Commerce Commission *v.* Inland Waterway Corporation, 319 U. S. 671 (1943).

[31] Four years later a similar case, Interstate Commerce Commission *v.* Mechling, 330 U. S. 567 (1947), came before the Court and this time Black was able to speak for a majority. He reaffirmed his position in the earlier case and the Court now refused to allow the establishment of rates favoring shipments made into Chicago by rail over those that had come part of the way by barge.

[32] 326 U. S. 60 (1945).

[33] *Ibid.,* p. 75.

[34] See McLean Trucking Co. *v.* United States, 321 U. S. 67 (1944); North Carolina *v.* United States, 325 U. S. 507 (1945); Interstate Commerce Commission *v.* Railway Labor Executives, 315 U. S. 373 (1942).

[35] 319 U. S. 491 (1943).

[36] 10 East 40th Street Building, Inc. *v.* Callus, 325 U. S. 578 (1945). It would appear that the majority of the Court has since accepted Black's position. See Martino *v.* Michigan Window Cleaning Co., 327 U. S. 173 (1946).

[37] Western Union Telegraph Co. *v.* Lenroot, 323 U. S. 490 (1945).

[38] Paul *v.* Virginia, 8 Wall. 168, 183 (1869).

[39] United States *v.* Southeastern Underwriters Association, 322 U. S. 533 (1944).

[40] 326 U. S. 572 (1946).

[41] California *v.* United States, 332 U. S. 19 (1947); United States *v.* Louisiana, 70 S. Ct. 914 (1950); United States *v.* Texas, 70 S. Ct. 918 (1950).

NOTES TO CHAPTER VII

[1] 311 U. S. 91 (1940).

[2] 325 U. S. 821 (1945).

[3] In his dissent Justice Jackson stated the matter thus: "There is no social interest served by union activities which are directed not to the advantage of union members but merely to capricious and retaliatory misuse of the power which unions have simply to impose their will on an employer. . . . The union cannot consistently with the Sherman Act refuse to enjoy the fruits of its victory and deny peace terms to an employer who has unconditionally surrendered." Hunt *v.* Crumboch, 325 U. S. 821, 829-831 (1945).

[4] 325 U. S. 797 (1945).

[5] "Congress never intended that unions could, consistently with the Sherman Act, aid non-labor groups to create business monopolies." Allen Bradley Co. *v.* Local Union No. 3, International Brotherhood of Electrical Workers, 325 U. S. 797, 808 (1945).

[6] United States *v.* United Mine Workers of America, 330 U. S. 258 (1947).

[7] United States *v.* Petrillo, 332 U. S. 1 (1947).

NOTES TO CHAPTER VII

[8] Lincoln Federal Labor Union *v.* Northwestern Iron and Metal Co., 335 U. S. 525 (1949). See also American Federation of Labor *v.* American Sash and Door Co., 335 U. S. 538 (1949).

[9] 312 U. S. 287 (1941). This was another case occasioned by the vendor system. In order to prevent independent vendors from departing from certain working standards that the union had been successful in establishing, union men resorted to violence on a considerable scale. Stores that dealt with independent vendors were set on fire, trucks were wrecked and bombs thrown. An Illinois court issued an injunction prohibiting all picketing which the Supreme Court thought was reasonable because the picketing had already been set in such a "background of violence" that the effect of the unlawful acts already committed would be projected by picketing even though no one engaged in further unlawful activities.

[10] *Ibid.*, p. 294.

[11] Giboney *v.* Empire Storage and Ice Co., 336 U. S. 490 (1949).

[12] Carpenters and Joiners Union *v.* Ritter's Cafe, 315 U. S. 722 (1942).

[13] International Brotherhood *v.* Hanke, 70 S. Ct. 773 (1950).

[14] Williams *v.* Jacksonville Terminal Company, 315 U. S. 386 (1942).

[15] *Ibid.*, pp. 410-411.

[16] XV, 592 (Eleventh Edition).

[17] *"Ad quaestionem legis respondent judices; ad quaestionem facti juratores."*

[18] See, "Trial," 64 *Corpus Juris*, pp. 296-508.

[19] *Ibid.*, pp. 310-312.

[20] See 2 *Lawyers Reports Annotated*, 340.

[21] See 64 *Corpus Juris*, 309.

[22] 319 U. S. 372 (1943).

[23] *Ibid.*, p. 401.

[24] Schuylkill and D. Improvement and Railroad Co. *v.* Munson, 14 Wallace 442 (1872).

[25] Galloway *v.* United States, 319 U. S. 372, 404-405 (1943). The case Black referred to was Gunning *v.* Cooley, 281 U. S. 90 (1929).

[26] *Ibid.*, p. 401.

[27] 320 U. S. 476 (1943).

[28] *Ibid.*, p. 484.

[29] See Stewart *v.* Southern Railroad Co., 315 U. S. 283 (1942); De Zon *v.* American President Lines, 318 U. S. 660 (1943); Wilkerson *v.* McCarthy, 336 U. S. 53 (1949).

[30] *Spoon River Anthology* (New York, 1922), p. 26. Quoted by permission of the author.

[31] 318 U. S. 54 (1943).

[32] *Ibid.*, p. 59.

[33] 320 U. S. 430 (1943).

[34] *Ibid.*, p. 442.

[35] *Ibid.*, p. 462.

[36] United Travelers *v.* Wolfe, 331 U. S. 586 (1947).

[37] Hawkins *v.* Barney, 5 Peters 457 (1831).

NOTES TO CHAPTER VII

[38] United Travelers *v.* Wolfe, 331 U. S. 586, 641-642 (1947).

[39] Williams *v.* North Carolina, 325 U. S. 226 (1945).

[40] See Federal Trade Commission *v.* Cement Institute, 333 U. S. 683 (1948); Mandeville Island Farms *v.* American Crystal Sugar Company, 334 U. S. 219 (1948); Schine Chain Theatres *v.* United States, 334 U. S. 110 (1948); United States *v.* Griffith, 334 U. S. 100 (1948); United States *v.* Paramount Pictures, 334 U. S. 131 (1948). Ford Motor Co. *v.* U. S. 335 U. S. 303 (1948).

[41] Associated Press *v.* United States, 326 U. S. 1 (1945).

[42] *Ibid.*, p. 20.

[43] See Temporary National Economic Committee, *Hearings on Concentration of Economic Power,* Part 2, *Patents* (1939).

[44] General Talking Pictures Corporation *v.* Western Electric Co., 305 U. S. 124 (1938).

[45] *Ibid.*, p. 127.

[46] *Ibid.*, p. 128.

[47] Williams Manufacturing Co. *v.* United Shoe Machinery Corp., 316 U. S. 364, 377 (1942).

[48] *Ibid.*, p. 393. See also his dissent in Mandel Bros. *v.* Wallace, 335 U. S. 291 (1948).

[49] 336 U. S. 271 (1949).

[50] Special Equipment Co. *v.* Coe, 324 U. S. 370, 383 (1945).

NOTES TO CHAPTER VIII

[1] Frank J. Wilson, "How We Trapped Capone," *Collier's,* April 26, 1947, p. 82.

[2] *The Republic* (New York, 1944), pp. 239-240.

[3] 309 U. S. 227 (1940).

[4] *Ibid.,* pp. 238-241.

[5] John A. Ryan, "Due Process and Mr. Justice Black," *Catholic World,* April, 1940, p. 38.

[6] Lisenba *v.* California, 314 U. S. 219 (1941).

[7] Ashcraft *v.* Tennessee, 322 U. S. 143 (1944).

[8] *Ibid.*, p. 154.

[9] 317 U. S. 269 (1942).

[10] Von Moltke *v.* Gillies, 332 U. S. 708, 720 (1948).

[11] *Ibid.*, p. 724. See also Quicksall *v.* Michigan, 70 S. Ct. 910 (1950).

[12] Barron *v.* Baltimore, 7 Peters 243, 247 (1833).

[13] See Near *v.* Minnesota, 283 U. S. 697 (1931); Palko *v.* Connecticut, 302 U. S. 319 (1937).

[14] Betts *v.* Brady, 316 U. S. 455, 474 (1942). In the case of Adamson *v.* California, 332 U. S. 46 (1947), he reaffirmed this position. California allowed the trial judge to comment to the jury on a defendant's failure to testify and allowed failure to testify to be considered as a probative fact. This practice was assailed as violative of the Fifth and Fourteenth Amendments in that its effect was to compel a witness to

testify against himself. The Supreme Court sustained the California procedure, declaring that the constitutional prohibition against compelling a witness to testify against himself applied only to the federal government. Justice Black, however, dissented and contended that the framers of the Fourteenth Amendment intended it to make applicable to the states the provisions of the entire Bill of Rights.

[15] Betts v. Brady, 316 U. S. 455, 476 (1942). See also Justice Murphy's dissenting opinion in which Justice Black concurred in the case of Bute v. Illinois, 333 U. S. 640 (1948).

[16] Avery v. Alabama, 308 U. S. 444 (1940).

[17] 327 U. S. 82 (1945).

[18] Ibid., p. 89.

[19] Tot v. United States, 319 U. S. 463 (1943). For other instances in which Black has voted against the constitutionality of acts of Congress see, United States v. Lovett, 328 U. S. 303 (1946); United Public Workers of America v. Mitchell, 330 U. S. 75 (1947); C. I. O. v. United States, 335 U. S. 106 (1948); American Communications Asso. v. Dowds, 70 S. Ct. 674 (1950).

[20] According to the statute the following groups of persons were ineligible for the "blue ribbon" juries: those who had been convicted of a criminal offense or found guilty of fraud or misconduct; those who possessed conscientious scruples against capital punishment; those who doubted their ability to lay aside an opinion or impression formed before the trial.

[21] Fay v. New York, 332 U. S. 261, 298 (1947). See also the dissenting opinion of Justice Murphy in which Justice Black concurred in Moore v. New York, 333 U. S. 565 (1948).

[22] Dennis v. United States, 70 S. Ct. 519 (1950).

[23] Ibid., p. 528.

[24] Akins v. Texas, 325 U. S. 398 (1945).

[25] See also Pierre v. Louisiana, 306 U. S. 354 (1939); Smith v. Texas, 311 U. S. 128 (1940); Cassell v. Texas, 70 S. Ct. 629 (1950).

[26] Duncan v. Kahanamoku, 327 U. S. 304 (1946).

[27] In 1942 the Attorney General of Hawaii submitted the following report to the Governor:

"In place of the criminal courts of this Territory there have been erected military commissions for the trial of all manner of offenses from the smallest misdemeanor to crimes carrying the death penalty. Trials have been conducted without regard to whether or not the subject matter is in any manner related to the prosecution of the war. These military tribunals are manned largely by army officers without legal training. Those who may have had any training in the law seem to have forgotten all they ever knew about the subject.

"Lawyers who appear before the tribunals are frequently treated with contempt and suspicion. Many citizens appear without counsel; they know, generally speaking, that no matter what evidence is produced the 'trial' will result in a conviction. An acquittal before these tribunals is a rare animal. Accordingly, in most cases a plea of guilty is entered in order to avoid the imposition of a more severe penalty. Those having the temerity to enter a plea of not guilty are dealt with more severely for having chosen that course. . . .

"The accused is not furnished with a copy of the charges against him but is permitted to examine the prosecutor's copy. . . . Cross examination of witnesses is tolerated with none too much patience by the court.

There have been instances in which arrests have been made and the accused kept in jail three or four days awaiting trial, even in the case of minor offenses. With the writ of *habeas corpus* suspended the unfortunate accused in such cases is without remedy. . . .

"The proceedings in these military tribunals are not only shocking to a lawyer but to anyone with a sense of fair play. Severe and bizarre sentences are meted out by persons untrained in the law. The feeling of the public is that they are guilty before they step inside the courtroom and their main problem is to escape with as light a sentence as possible." John P. Frank, "Ex Parte Milligan *v.* The Five Companies; Martial Law in Hawaii," *Columbia Law Review* (September, 1944), XLIV, 652-653.

[28] 4 Wallace 2 (1866).

[29] *Ibid.*, p. 127.

[30] Duncan *v.* Kahanamoku, 327 U. S. 304, 322 (1946).

[31] 70 S. Ct. 936 (1950).

[32] Johnson *v.* Eisentrager, 70 S. Ct. 953 (1950).

NOTES TO CHAPTER IX

[1] Robert M. McIver, *The Web of Government* (New York, 1947), p. 203.

[2] Thus Professor E. S. Corwin, a veteran scholar in the field of Constitutional Law, has accused it upon occasion of "obvious departure from common sense and common law." *The Constitution and What It Means Today* (8th ed., Princeton, 1946), Preface, p. ix.

[3] Milkwagon Drivers Union *v.* Meadowmoor Dairies, 312 U. S. 287, 301-302 (1941).

[4] 316 U. S. 584 (1942).

[5] Jones *v.* Opelika, 319 U. S. 103 (1943); Murdock *v.* Pennsylvania, 319 U. S. 105 (1943).

[6] 319 U. S. 141 (1943).

[7] *Ibid.*, p. 146.

[8] *Ibid.*, pp. 146-147.

[9] A further example is furnished by the case of Saia *v.* New York, 334 U. S. 558 (1948), in which the Court held that a municipal ordinance regulating the use of sound trucks unconstitutionally deprived a member of the Jehovah's Witnesses of his freedom of speech and religion. Justice Black was among the five members of the Court who constituted a majority.

[10] 326 U. S. 501 (1946).

[11] *Ibid.*, pp. 506-509.

Notes to Chapter IX

[12] 321 U. S. 158 (1944).

[13] 330 U. S. 1 (1947).

[14] The prohibition of the First Amendment against the establishment of a religion has been made applicable to state action by the interpretation which incorporates it in the due process clause of the Fourteenth Amendment.

[15] Everson v. Board of Education, 330 U. S. 1, 18 (1947).

[16] *Ibid.,* p. 19.

[17] *Ibid.,* p. 18.

[18] McCollum v. Board of Education, 333 U. S. 203 (1948).

[19] *Ibid.* See Justice Frankfurter's concurring opinion.

[20] Everson v. Board of Education, 330 U. S. 1, 15 (1947).

[21] In Minersville School District v. Gobitis, 310 U. S. 586 (1940) Black voted with the majority of the Court to uphold a state law requiring school children to give the pledge of allegiance to the flag although certain students claimed that to take part in such a ceremony violated their religious scruples and hence deprived them of their religious freedom. Several years later Black joined the majority of the Court in striking down a similar law, candidly admitting that he now believed such a law unconstitutional and that his original judgment had been erroneous. West Virginia State Board of Euducation v. Barnette, 319 U. S. 624 (1943).

[22] Bridges v. California, 314 U. S. 252 (1941).

[23] *Ibid.,* p. 263.

[24] .Thomas v. Collins, 323 U. S. 516 (1945).

[25] United States v. Congress of Industrial Organizations, 335 U. S. 106 (1948).

[26] In connection with the freedom of speech see Justice Black's opinions in cases involving the right to picket, Chapter VII, pp. 111-113.

[27] American Communications Association v. Douds, 70 S. Ct. 674 (1950).

[28] *Ibid.,* p. 683.

[29] *Ibid.,* p. 709.

[30] *Idem.*

[31] *Ibid.,* p. 711.

[32] United Public Workers of America v. Mitchell, 330 U. S. 75 (1947).

[33] *Ibid.,* p. 111.

[34] See Missouri *ex rel.* Gaines v. Canada, 305 U. S. 337 (1938); Sipuel *v.* University of Oklahoma, 332 U. S. 631 (1948); Fisher v. Hurst, 333 U. S. 147 (1948); Sweatt v. Painter, 70 S. Ct. 848 (1950).

[35] McLaurin v. Oklahoma State Regents, 70 S. Ct. 851 (1950).

[36] Mitchell v. United States, 313 U. S. 80 (1941); Henderson v. United States, 70 S. Ct. 843 (1950).

[37] Morgan v. Virginia, 328 U. S. 373 (1946).

[38] Shelley v. Kraemer, 334 U. S. 1 (1948).

[39] Korematsu v. United States, 323 U. S. 214 (1944).

[40] *Ibid.,* p. 220.

[41] *Ibid.,* p. 233.

[42] Oyama v. California, 332 U. S. 633 (1948).

[43] Takahashi *v.* Fish and Game Commission, 334 U. S. 410 (1948).

[44] 325 U. S. 1 (1945).

[45] Knauer *v.* United States, 328 U. S. 654 (1946).

[46] *Ibid.*, pp. 674-675.

[47] John Henry Wigmore, *A Treatise on the System of Evidence in Trials at Common Law* (Boston, 1905), IV, 2954.

[48] United States *v.* Di Re, 332 U. S. 581 (1948).

[49] Johnson *v.* United States, 333 U. S. 10 (1948).

[50] Trupiano *v.* United States, 334 U. S. 699 (1948).

[51] *Idem.*

[52] United States *v.* Rabinowitz, 70 S. Ct. 430 (1950).

[53] 338 U. S. 74 (1949).

NOTES TO CHAPTER X

[1] In 1930, for example, only 11 per cent of the Court's opinions were non-unanimous; in 1936, 19 per cent were non-unanimous; while in 1946, 64 per cent were non-unanimous. See C. Herman Pritchett, *The Roosevelt Court* (New York, 1948), p. 25.

[2] This cartoon, published originally in the New York *Herald Tribune,* is reproduced in Wesley McCune's *The Nine Young Men* (New York, 1947) p. 44.

[3] See "Divisions of Opinion Among Justices of the United States Supreme Court, 1939-1941," *American Political Science Review* (October, 1941), XXXV, 890; "Ten Years of Supreme Court Voting," *Southwestern Social Science Quarterly* (June, 1943), XXIV, 12; "The Divided Supreme Court, 1944-1945," *Michigan Law Review* (December, 1945), XLIV, 427; "The Roosevelt Court: Votes and Values," *American Political Science Review* (February, 1948), XLIII, 53. Most of the material in these articles has been included in Professor Pritchett's book, *The Roosevelt Court.*

[4] Federal Power Commission *v.* Hope Natural Gas Co., 320 U. S. 591, 619 (1944).

[5] Securities and Exchange Commission *v.* Chenery Corporation, 332 U. S. 194, 214 (1947).

[6] See the tables prepared by Pritchett in *The Roosevelt Court,* pp. 242-247.

[7] *Ibid.,* p. 247.

[8] Harold Ickes, "My Twelve Years with F. D. R.," *Saturday Evening Post,* July 17, 1948, p. 98.

[9] New York *Times,* April 29, 1946.

[10] Ickes, *Saturday Evening Post,* July 3, 1948, p. 88.

[11] *Ibid.*

[12] For the full text of Jackson's letter see New York *Times,* June 11, 1946.

[13] May 16, 1946.

[14] New York *Times,* June 14, 1946.

NOTES TO CHAPTER X

[15] Jewell Ridge Coal Corporation *v.* Local No. 6147, United Mine Workers of America, 325 U. S. 897 (1945).

[16] Jewell Ridge Coal Corporation *v.* Local No. 6167, United Mine Workers of America, 325 U. S. 161 (1945).

[17] Jewell Ridge Coal Corporation *v.* Local No. 6167, United Mine Workers of America, 325 U. S. 897 (1945).

[18] New York *Herald Tribune,* June 12, 1946.

[19] New York *Times,* June 11, 1946.

[20] *Ibid.,* June 12, 1946.

[21] *Congressional Record,* June 12, 1946, p. 6723.

[22] Senate Joint Resolution 167, 79th Cong., 2d. sess.

[23] *P. M.,* June 12, 1946.

[24] "High Court Controversy," *New Republic,* June 24, 1946, p. 887.

[25] "The Supreme Court, 1947," *Fortune,* January, 1947, p. 78.

[26] Ickes, *Saturday Evening Post,* July 3, 1948, p. 88.

[27] For example Chief Justice Stone sat on the Court when members of his former law firm of Sullivan and Cromwell argued the case of North American Company *v.* Securities and Exchange Commission, 327 U. S. 686 (1946), and Justice Roberts did not feel called upon to disqualify himself when certain of his old clients appeared before the Court as litigants. Although he had represented both the Pennsylvania Railroad Company and the Bell Telephone Company, he took part in the decisions of Georgia *v.* Pennsylvania Railroad Company, 324 U. S. 439 (1945) and Bell Telephone Company *v.* Pennsylvania Public Utility Commission, 309 U. S. 30 (1940). Likewise Justice Butler sat in the case of Great Northern Railroad Company *v.* Washington, 300 U. S. 154 (1937) although he had represented that railroad before his appointment to the Supreme Court.

[28] In twelve instances Justice Black wrote lone dissents and in three others where other justices also dissented he wrote separate opinions. Justices Reed and Jackson each wrote four single dissents.

[29] He dissented six times in the company of Frankfurter and Jackson and three more times with Frankfurter alone.

NOTE TO CONCLUSION

[1] Justice Cardozo has stated his position thus: "I think that when a rule, after it has been duly tested by experience, has been found to be inconsistent with the sense of justice or with the social welfare, there should be less hesitation in frank avowal and full abandonment." *The Nature of the Judicial Process* (New Haven, 1921), p. 150. Professor Samuel Williston has written: "If the precedent is an outlaw it should be shot in full view of the public, rather than lured to the operating room and put to sleep by an overdose of judicial anaesthesia. Nobody can be sure that such sleep is permanent." *Some Modern Tendencies in the Law* (New York, 1929), p. 86.

INDEX

205

DATE DUE

GAYLORD			PRINTED IN U.S.A.